ABOUT THE AUTHOR

Arthur Allwright began his writing career at the age of seventy. At the insistence of his grandchildren, he produced his first striking work, answering their question, "What was it like, being an evacuee during the Second World War?" "A Stranger And Afraid" tells subsequent generations what it was like to be an eight- year-old stranger in an even stranger land for three years with a Quaker family in Somerset. You should make time to read that book!

The publication of the book inspired him to join a Kent-based group of writers, who turned his interests to short story writing and poetry. Many of those short stories were contained in his second published book, "Time For A Quickie", (Short Stories For Busy People).

He enjoys sharing his experiences and stories with school groups and communities. The natural progression is to share some more of his memories with you.

By the same author

A STRANGER AND AFRAID
(A true story of the author's wartime evacuation)

ISBN 1-904224-31-8

TIME FOR A QUICKIE
(Short Stories for Busy People)

ISBN 978-1-84923-166-4

FOR KING, COUNTRY
and the
LOVE OF ANN

By Arthur Allwright

To Mike,

I hope you enjoy my contribution to history.

Best Wishes

Arth Allwright

19th September, 2013.

Copyright page

First published in 2010 by YouWriteOn Publishing
Copyright Text Arthur Allwright

First Edition

The author asserts the moral right under the Copyright, Designs and Patents Act 1988 to be identified as the author of this work.

All rights reserved. No part of this publication may be reproduced, stored in a retrieval system, or transmitted, in any form or by any means without the prior written consent of the author, nor be otherwise circulated in any form of binding or cover other than that in which it is published and without a similar condition being imposed on the subsequent purchaser.

British Library C. I. P.

A CIP catalogue record for this title is available from the British Library.

INTRODUCTION

Immediately after the Second World War there was still a need for our armed forces to be present around the world. In addition, the cold war relationship between Russia and the West led our government to introduce National Service for young men to serve eighteen months, later, two years, in one of the three armed Services.

The author of "For King, Country and the Love of Ann" served in the Royal Air Force from March 1949. Those were the days when youngsters respected their elders and couples went to the altar as virgins.

But National Service produced a grave problem for the author. At eighteen years old he was deeply in love with Ann. The daily letters that flowed between them enables the author to capture his endeavours to retain Ann's love for him whilst he served the King.

Ann and Arthur 1949

PROLOGUE

1948 was a good year; a year of unplanned change. I was still at school, studying for the Higher Schools Certificate prior to attending Goldsmiths Teachers Training College due to commence in 1949. My parents' situation meant that a university education was never a possibility. As a seventeen year-old sportsman with aspirations of being a schoolteacher, I had enjoyed the added security of a steady girl friend, Bessie, for three years. My home life consisted of having somewhere to sleep. We were not a close family unit, mainly because, at the age of eight I had been evacuated to Somerset for nearly four years. Consequently, after the war, I was seldom at home, seeking entertainment wherever I could find it..

On July 5th 1948 I called at Bessie's house to take her to our regular Monday evening excitement at Wimbledon speedway. We argued about two tickets that I had acquired for the following evening, to see Arthur Askey at the Empire, Kingston-upon-Thames. The result was that I went to the speedway alone, joining a group of about thirty supporters who always stood together. My plan was to find a companion for the Tuesday, and I was delighted when my offer of a theatre date was accepted by a girl who I had never seen before.

It was not a very good start to a relationship. I arranged to meet the tall slim smiling girl at Raynes Park station for the journey to Kingston, but I had forgotten her name. The forgiving nature of Ann, however, was reflected in our enjoyment of the outing. We laughed throughout the show and, not wanting to appear too forward, I walked her home without attempting to kiss her. Her acceptance of another date sent me home in high spirits and on the following day I told Bessie that we were finished. I never saw her again.

Three months later, Goldsmiths confirmed that I must complete my compulsory national service before joining their college. My priorities immediately changed in favour of earning money and I left school, accepting a post of temporary clerk with the Inland Revenue.

The sudden access to an income to supplement my paper-round money, albeit small, enabled me to pay my way with Ann, who had

viii

embarked on a couture dress-making career. She inspired confidence in me and we found ourselves completely in love. Her elder sister Margaret and her parents treated me as family, and I experienced warmth in their welcome whenever I visited their home.

The impending break in our relationship became a reality when my joining –up papers arrived in February, 1949. The strength of our loyalty would be put to the test while serving in the Royal Air Force, starting on 30th March, 1949.

FOR KING, COUNTRY AND THE LOVE OF ANN

CHAPTER 1

"Spell out my name, airman."

"It's Corporal Preston, spelt, P-R-E-S-T-O-N."

"No it's not," screamed the irate Irish corporal, crashing his cane onto his desk, making us all jump with fear. "When I ask you in future to spell my name, you spell it like this, B-A-S-T-A-R-D."

Forty grown men immediately became inert and dumb. The jocular banter that had greeted the corporal as he emerged from his tiny room at the end of the hut had died embarrassingly as his fierce features stunned his audience. We recognised the corporal as the animal whose reputation had preceded him. We had heard rumours about him at Padgate. Corporal Preston would be our tormentor during our eight weeks of 'square bashing' training at RAF West Kirby in The Wirral, Cheshire. My world had suddenly clouded over. I realised that this bully would stop at nothing to ensure that this Flight would be the leading group at the passing-out parade. He was hell-bent on destroying us as human beings.

Two hundred national service eighteen year old recruits had been welcomed into the RAF at Padgate, in Cheshire seven days earlier. All of us had either just left school when our 'Call-up' papers arrived, or had enjoyed no more than six months work experience. It was 1949 and national service satisfied a need to supplement the armed forces after the end of the Second World War. It was not optional, except that youths could choose to join any of the armed services.

A camaraderie had surfaced amongst us on arrival at Padgate. None of us wanted to be there. Most of us were in the early planning stage of our careers. I intended to be a school teacher and had been accepted by the Goldsmiths Teachers Training College, New Cross, in London. But suddenly, I was notified that the national service had to be completed before the training could commence. The greatest upheaval for us was that we all had to leave families and loved ones at home, not knowing how often we might see each other. As a boy, I had been evacuated from my family twice during the war, but for many of the men this was the first experience of being away from home, even for one night.

My sadness centred around missing my girlfriend, Ann. Our young love had blossomed for nearly a year and although we were not officially engaged, we talked endlessly about our future lives together. Neither of us could boast of any financial stability in our respective families, so we would be dependent on promotion at work to bring our hopes to fruition. Ann was in the rag trade and my working career would not start until after my RAF days. Achieving our ambitions would be dependant, therefore, on the sincerity of our love, and luck. The fear of losing Ann whilst I was away had begun nibbling at my brain, even on the journey to Padgate.

The parting at Euston station in London had been tearful. The brave faces that we portrayed on the journey from home to London were false, a façade to give the impression of adulthood. Ann had taken a day's leave to wave good-bye, but perhaps this had not been a good decision. We stood on the platform with nothing to say. For the umpteenth time I said that I would write as soon as I had the address, and Ann responded that she would write back immediately. We were not alone. Three other couples were eating each other as a means of showing the intensity of their love for each other. As the shrill whistle sounded, we all indulged in a final burst of passion and withdrew through our respective doors. I surreptitiously wiped my eyes before sitting next to one of the lads in a similar situation. We consoled each other by engaging in meaningless chatter about our backgrounds, but we sensed that it was unlikely that we would be housed together, based on the large number of look-alikes travelling North.

30th March, 1949

My Own Dearest Ann,
Well, I'm here darling, but I don't realise it yet ! I cannot get it into my big head that I shall not be seeing you tonight after your Girls' Training Corps. I was so sad leaving you yesterday, after you had given me such a wonderful afternoon. I cannot thank you enough for the lovely biro that I'm using to write telling you how much I love you.

Everyone here seems cheerful so I don't want you to worry darling. My only purpose here is for the RAF to make a man out of me – good enough for you to live with for ever.
My address here is :-
Intake No. 190, Hut 176, Flight D4
No. 1 Reception Unit,
RAF Padgate, Nr. Warrington, Lancs.

When we arrived at Warrington, covered lorries with benches inside, took us to the camp. We were allocated to long huts, twenty men to a hut. Two sheets, two blankets and a hard pillow were already folded on each bed and you could choose any spot. Stupid me, I chose to sleep next to a lad who snores.
I'll write as soon as possible. Please be happy sweetheart,
From your loving husband-to-be,
Arthur.

Within the first week I had already learned one of the greatest advantages of national service, that of comradeship. We could either muck-in and help each other to survive, or rebel against the system and pay the price. Even in the short time that we had been together, I could point to certain lads who were hell-bent on causing trouble for themselves by not accepting the inevitable. I chose the former option and was determined to try and enjoy the enforced disciplined environment even though it meant being separated from my heart-throb girlfriend.

A second lesson was close behind. None of us had any money, and I discovered that food acquisition would be a popular ingredient in the bonding of friendships. Rationing was still prevalent and although working in the cookhouse wasn't attractive, it had its merits when we could take feasts back to the billet for sharing after 'lights out'. Our hut was allocated the cookhouse 'fatigues' jobs on the third day. We were told to split into three shifts, 5am to 10am, 11am to 3pm and 4pm to 9pm. The corporal in charge of our hut chose six nearest the door to do the early shift, on the grounds that when the wake-up call arrived there would be a minimum of disturbance for the remainder of the hut. As it turned out, the early risers made such a commotion, nobody slept any more. I clicked for the evening duty which suited me as I didn't want to spend any money in the NAAFI. The main cooked meal for the day was served from 12 noon to 2pm and the evening tea usually consisted of something on toast, followed by bread and jam and anything left over from dinner. We discovered that the full-time cookhouse staff had their meal after the tea things had been cleared away and washed up, and enjoyed the freedom of choice of menu.

The cookhouse sergeant, whose size reflected the number of years that he had served in catering, gave a tempting description of life in the catering side of the air force.

"Just think lads, when the officers at your training camp ask you to decide in which branch of the service you want to perform, you now know what to say. You'll get all the training you'll ever want to set up your own café when you get demobbed. And, you'll be everyone's friend. Even the officers are afraid to pull rank on you. They all love their bellies too much."

One of the early Padgate tasks was to queue for our kit that would last for the eighteen months: a kitbag endorsed with our name and service number; a back-pack; one pair of boots; 3 pairs of socks and underwear; 4 shirts plus collars and studs; one black tie; working uniform; best blue uniform; 2 berets or forage caps; one greatcoat, which had to be worn or carried from 1st October to 30th April and not otherwise; rain cape; one mug and cutlery; and most important, a 'housewife', the pack of needles, thread and buttons. The tailor took two days to make the changes to the uniforms, after which the wearing of the full uniform was mandatory whilst on duty.

31st March, 1949

My Darling Arthur,
Your letter has arrived so quickly and has helped me get over the first few days of being parted from you. As I write this letter, Donald Peers is singing 'Far Away Places'. It must be for us, but it makes me feel so sad. I love you so much and I want you home with me.

Mum has just read a story in the paper that the Church in the Woods at Hastings caught fire yesterday but the firemen saved it from too much damage. It is that lovely church that we visited last month when we went to Hastings for our lovely time together. Hastings will always be my favourite place because of our memories of Bottle Alley and the wonky slope of the floor between our two rooms in the guest house.
Please don't ever stop loving me.
All my love for ever,
Ann.

Some of the intake were destined to remain at Padgate for their eight weeks 'square bashing', but our three huts were allocated to West Kirby. The transfer to our new camp was accompanied by rain and high winds. The lorry that arrived to take the kitbags to the station two miles away coughed and spluttered, but refused to start and the sergeant exercised his sense of humour by telling us that we would have to carry the kitbags to the station. Padgate Station turned out to be two platforms with no cover and the hour wait for the train did nothing for our morale. A further wait in the rain at Liverpool Station brought a little amusement when two elderly ladies approached the sergeant.

"Why can't you let those poor boys shelter under the roof instead of making them get wet? Your mother would be ashamed of you!"

"He hasn't got a mother", came from the ranks, followed by general laughter.

The sergeant reacted without a smile. "Airmen, fall-out, take shelter with your fairy godmothers! Do not leave the platform."

Eventually, we moved to the Underground, taking a train under the Mersey and across The Wirral to West Kirby Station. The welcome sight of a lorry for the kitbags was the only good news.

"It's three miles to the camp and you'll now get some marching practice. Get fell in". Obviously, the corporal sent to meet us, was well educated. "A band will escort us from the top of the hill."

But the band had other things to do, because they didn't turn up. Instead, we made our own music by whistling tunes that many of the marchers had rude words to suit. The camp gates could never have been more welcome, as the crocodile of tired and bedraggled airmen came to attention outside three huts that were to be our home and refuge from the Irish Sea gales for three months.

"You can see the sea on two sides of the camp and there is nothing to stop the winds from America to West Kirby. You'll find out!" Perhaps the flight sergeant hadn't heard of Ireland, but nobody intended arguing with him. We just wanted to collect our kitbags, unpack and find the cookhouse for tea. Then, bed would be the priority, just to dream of our loved ones.

We were learning fast, however, and in the RAF things do not have to run smoothly, like night following day and going to bed when you are tired. Oh no. Bastards like Corporal Preston can influence the universe. We were about to discover that Corporal Preston could make grown men cry.

Morning arrived with a bang, literally. I was about to cross red traffic lights on my bicycle in my dreams, when the whole of the Wirral was awakened by Preston and his rendering of Silent Night using a bucket and his cane. Our feet hit the deck before our eyes had a chance of establishing whether or not it was yet daylight. It wasn't.

"Ablutions at the double, come on," he roared. "Then, outside in threes at six thirty. What's this I see?"

Jim, two beds up from me, had dared to stay under the clothes. In a flash, the iron bedstead rose into the air in the dimly-lit hut and crashed onto the naked torso that had beaten the bed to the floor by a millisecond. Two other lucky airmen further up the hut, witnessed the display and applied discretion just in time. Unfortunately, one of them still boasted a morning erection and paid the hefty price of a whack with the cane.

When I returned from the ablutions, Jim was still groaning, lying on his bed having his back massaged by his mate who said that he knew about these things. The mate then had the courage to face Preston, whose only comment was that Jim would have to wait till 9am for sick parade. As it happened, all of us were detailed to attend sick parade to have our vaccination marks, pinned on us at Padgate, inspected. Three of us whose arms were slightly swollen were excused marching for twenty four hours, which saved us from two hours of drilling in a gale. Corporal Preston was not amused. He sent the other two to clean the ablutions while I had to sweep and polish his room. The back-handed reward for doing a reasonable job was that I was made 'Recruit Leader' for the hut, which meant that I acted as a go-between the men and the corporal and got the nick-name 'Crawler'. Meanwhile, Jim remained in the camp hospital for two days, which prompted the threat from Preston that unless Jim caught up with the training, he would be re-flighted, staying an extra week at West Kirby. Nobody in their right mind would want that!

There was no marching on the third day. Instead we were treated to a series of organisational niceties about the RAF. With the rank of AC2 we were promised £1 per week for the duration of the time at West Kirby. Any assignments thereafter for Trade Training would attract 7s.6d per day. Increases would depend on promotion. We could elect to have 9d per day stopped from our pay to finance travel warrants when we had home leave. A question about leave brought the fantastic news that we would all get three days leave for Easter. My brain was spinning with plans to make sure that Ann would be available.

I noticed that the three speakers during the sessions were young pilot officers, the lowest officer rank, and one of them volunteered the information that they were national servicemen and that we could apply for consideration to undergo officer training. Another pilot officer was the Sports Officer for the camp and he wanted cross-country runners to train and take part in competitive runs on behalf of the camp. The officer possibility had pound sign attractions and the volunteering for cross–country runs could be a means of escaping marching periods. I collected the necessary forms and felt quite smug. But all was not well. On my return to the hut, I discovered that volunteering brought its own stigma. The majority of the airmen preferred to 'rough it' if the alternative was to work with officers.

That evening, sleep was hindered by the conflict between comradeship and the pounds, shillings and pence for my future with Ann.

8

CHAPTER 2

Sleep proved to be a good settler of problems. By the morning I had made up my mind to match the headlines of the News Chronicle, 'Grim and Bear It'. I signed up with the education section to attend Advanced Maths and French lessons on Monday evenings and Geography for an hour on Tuesday evenings. I needed to keep up the momentum for studying if I wanted the Goldsmiths Teacher Training College offer to become a reality.

Daytimes had already been mapped out for us. Square-bashing had started with a vengeance. All over the large parade square, which was about the size of two football pitches, groups of thirty airmen marched endlessly up and down and across the square. Every group had its own corporal screaming at his fledglings. The low-peaked caps of the corporals gave them an air of authority and being armed with a cane and blessed with voices that ejected decibels higher than those of ordinary human beings, they were a force to be respected.

We were taught to stand to attention with fists clenched and thumbs to the front; head up, chin in and shoulders back. We marched at a thirty two inch pace and our clenched fists were thrust forward, level with our shoulders Within a couple of days we could 'size off in threes' and march in a reasonably smart fashion, or so we thought.

"Why can't you remember to start off with your bloody left foot?" boomed Corporal Preston, one morning. "Do it once more, Murphy, and you'll be back tonight."

Poor old Murphy just couldn't co-ordinate his feet and arms and instead of leading with his left foot and right arm, if his left foot went forward, so did his left arm. The corporal allowed one or two jibes from the ranks before treading on Murphy's left foot.

"Now remember. Lead off with the foot that hurts."

Murphy was more concerned with the damage that the corporal had done to the polish on his boot and shouted abuse.

"Ok, so you all think it's funny. We'll all meet at six tonight to have a boot polishing lesson. Then, perhaps we'll learn not to waste our marching time."

The other marching groups had all been dismissed for the NAAFI tea break five minutes before we ended our session. We wondered what else the corporal had up his sleeves for punishments. On our arrival in the NAAFI there was a buzz of excitement. Administrative information and orders relating to the camp were published as Station Routine Orders, or SROs. The latest notice gave the news that we had all been waiting for … five days leave for Easter, starting Thursday, could be taken subject to a successful application for a Pass which would have to be carried at all times. The education class that afternoon concentrated on the discipline necessary for all airmen on leave. Best blue uniform with highly polished buttons must be worn, to and from camp. When in uniform, officers of any of the services must be saluted.

"Even in a public toilet?" called out Jim

"Anywhere," replied the instructor, "but be careful with what you may have in your hand."

We were warned that the RAF Military Police roamed the cities and would arrest any airman misbehaving or being improperly dressed. They wore peaked caps with a white band, earning them a nickname of 'snowdrops'.

My main concern was to let Ann know that I would be home on the Thursday evening and to ensure that she would free over the weekend. I could phone her only if I had made a prior arrangement for her to be in the next door neighbours' house at a given time. The neighbours, Mr. and Mrs. Diamond were two of the few people in the street with a telephone, Malden 2692. The safest way was to send a telegram, which could be done from the camp post office.

Post Office Telegram. 12th April,1949

Ann Cobbett 59, Greenway, London, SW20
Arriving Thursday Evening Love Arthur

The boot polishing exercise proved to be an eye-opener. Although we thought that we were getting quite a shine on the toecaps, Corporal Preston had other ideas.

"When you've shined the buggers, you apply another layer of Cherry Blossom and rub it in with the back of a teaspoon. Keep rubbing in a circle and then buff it up with your cloth. Then start again, and again, till you can see me in them, breathing down your neck on the parade ground."

Wednesday had been a horrible day. The programme listed it as Sports Day. What we hadn't realised was that immediately after breakfast the PE instructor gave us fifteen minutes to line up in threes outside the huts, wearing plimsolls, shorts and vest. There had been a late frost and the sports were scheduled for the West Kirby beach. After three miles of gentle running, down the hill and through the town, where the early locals offered us unwelcome advice, we arrived on the sand, shattered and sweating. We were split into four teams for football and rounders. I immediately learned another lesson about keeping my mouth shut.

"Who gets on well with his mother-in-law?" called the instructor.

"I do." I replied, instinctively, thinking about Ann's mum who I thought was lovely.

"Ok. Your team can remove your vests." Again I was not scoring in the popularity stakes.

The cold Atlantic and Irish Sea winds bit into our bodies and to demonstrate his sense of humour, the instructor gave our team the onerous job of playing against the wind. I had never seen so much sand. We could only imagine that the sea was at the distant horizon, but none of us was in the mood for paddling. After an hour of uncontrolled arguing and shouting we were allowed the doubtful pleasure of a ten minute break, still in the biting wind. Then, back to camp, running to the foot of the hill and marching the remainder of the way.

The afternoon lecture centred on a subject that surprised us, venereal disease. Having established that about twenty out of the hundred present had 'gone all the way' with girls, the doctor showed a fifteen minute colour film of ghastly images of people suffering from the disease. The airmen who had boasted at the beginning of the talk were decidedly subdued after the film. We were then warned against dating the 'camp followers', prostitutes who waited outside the various RAF and army posts. There was laughter when the doctor ended with the news that Durex could be obtained free from the medical centre for those who couldn't keep their powder dry.

There was one little problem with going on leave on a Thursday. Wednesday night was 'Housewives' Night'. No, there were no visitors to keep us happy, just a name for preparing the huts for weekly inspection. Our fears surrounded that self-styled bastard, Preston. We knew that he had no home to visit for Easter and would be staying on camp. Nobody would choose to keep him company! The one advantage for me was that, as Recruit Leader, I had an easier task to encourage the others to add a lot more spit and polish to ensure that he didn't carry out his threat of delaying our departure for home until the cleaning was done to his satisfaction.

Thursday arrived, bringing an air of excitement to the hut. Men were whistling in the ablution block. I noticed that each man was being particularly careful about cleaning his basin after washing and shaving, ensuring that the whole area would be acceptably for the inspection. The bogs, that were often untenable and smelly, were spotless. Jokes abounded. There were no defaulters on the breakfast parade and surprise, surprise, nobody reported sick. On our return from the cookhouse we waited expectantly for the orderly officer to inspect the billet. Last minute tidying up was done willingly and Jim gave the polished lino a quick rub with the 'bumper' to remove signs of the morning footprints. Surely the room would pass the test. Corporal Preston kept a low profile; it was suggested that he was still in bed. Others thought that he had gone on leave Wednesday evening without saying 'Good Bye'. There was no volunteer to open his door to find out.

At 10.30 the admin clerk arrived with the Leave Passes and the news that the inspection had been cancelled and that lorries would leave for the railway station at 11.15. Pandemonium broke out as we rushed to change into our best blue uniforms for the dash home. I had been away from Ann for less than three weeks but it had been an eternity. All that remained was to have an uneventful journey, but the railway gremlins were not on our side. The steam train from Glasgow limped into Liverpool, with no heating and no empty seats. The guard beckoned a group of us to join him in the guard's van, which already had become a home for two cages of cats that smelled worse than Corporal Preston's breath. But we were able to spread out on the floor without getting our tunics dirty. Unfortunately the engine was thirsty and stopped for water at Crewe and Rugby and we arrived at Euston one hour late, very tired and sore.

The midnight hour was about to chime when I rang the bell at No.59, Greenway, hoping that Ann's parents wouldn't be too cross for the lateness of the call. But it was all smiles. The uniform came in for special attention and I had to promise to wear it the following day for the old Brownie reflex camera to do its job.

Ann had bought tickets to attend the Crusaders Boys Club dance on the Saturday evening. In her mind, this would be the opportunity to show me off in my uniform. I was embarrassed with the attention shown but it was wonderful, holding Ann close without treading on her toes with my large boots. The dance had cheered up Ann and we continually stopped for another last kiss on our way home.

There was just too much to fit into the weekend. My own family wanted to hear my story and my sisters were unusually vocative. Tuesday arrived too soon, with the inevitable tearful farewell on Euston platform for the 6pm train. It was another six hour journey to Liverpool and to pass the time, I started another letter to Ann, the tenth in three weeks. But writing on my lap with a jerky train did not help. Several of us managed to catch the last train to West Kirby and it was a cold walk to camp where things went from bad to worse.

"Into the guardroom, airmen. You are all two hours late. Your passes expired at midnight." The sergeant busied himself with completing the Charge Sheets Form 252, ignoring the pleas and weak excuses being thrown at him.

"Report here at 7am to be formally charged."

Some people have no difficulty injecting unhappiness into situations and I had discovered in the last month that the RAF specialised in breeding characters to do just that. In order to appear at the guardroom next morning, properly dressed, we had to miss breakfast. The orderly officer who took the parade, however, was unlike the sergeant and listened to our garbled accounts of the misdemeanours of the train and its late arrival in Liverpool. He nodded in agreement and politely pointed out that in future it would be prudent to get an earlier train to prevent aggravation. I gained the impression that he felt genuinely sorry that we had been put through the ignominy of being charged so early in our career.

"You will be getting 48-hour passes in three weeks time for Whitsun so bear in mind what I've told you. Charges dismissed."

We couldn't believe our ears. Somebody had spoken to us with a civil tongue and the news about Whitsun gave us some good news to take back to the hut.

Sat 23rd April, 1949

My Darling Arthur,
It was so lovely to hear your voice on the telephone last night. The second three minutes were much clearer than the first three. And I have your new photo on my machine at work. I look at you all day. On

Friday, Eva pretended to tear it up because they are fed up with me talking about you.
Tonight, I feel lonely, sitting with Mum alone. Dad is at Gran's, who is very ill. Mum has been saying such nice things about you and I feel so proud that you are mine. She never talks of people like that. I love you so much.
All my love for ever,
Ann.

Week four of our training schedule had mixed surprises in store. Interviews with the Careers Officer were arranged and these were preceded by a lecture on the opportunities available. National service had advantages for those who had not mapped out their career and the aim was to teach a trade to everyone who wanted it. Driving lessons were available for budding lorry drivers, and vehicle maintenance in the Motor Transport Sections would add useful experience. The Catering Corp offered chef training, coupled with the financial planning of the cookhouse. Electricians, plumbers, carpenters, P E instructors and administration staff had special courses. Aircrew opportunities for officers and ground crew training for other ranks were available. But none of these were attractive to me. Instead, I noticed that a lot of emphasis was being given to a new-fangled occupation surrounding Radar. One good plus point was that most radar sites were small and self-contained, and I remembered the advice from an old schoolmaster about being a big fish in a small pool, rather than being a small fish in a big pool.

At my interview the officer had experience of radar control and painted a rosy picture of life in that area. Fighter plotting was a segment of radar work and seemed to be more fun than getting strained eyes by sitting for hours in front of a brightly lit radar screen. The job of a fighter plotter was sold to me and I was told to expect my eight week training to take place at Bawdsey in Suffolk at the end of my square-bashing.

The bad news was that rifle training started in week four and each of us signed for a rifle, knowing that we were responsible for its safety and maintenance. It was heavy and awkward to manipulate. Corporal Preston greeted us back on the parade square with our acquisitions.

"You will now get to know what its like to be tired. They made these toys heavy, just for you. First of all, you'll learn how to carry them, standing to attention. How to shoulder arms, how to salute with them and how to march will come later. Then comes the bit I like. We'll start tonight at 8pm learning how to clean them."

He was right. Two hours of solid introductory drill followed.

"All the drill movements will be done to numbers. Stand to attention with your toy resting on the ground with its heel alongside your right boot, trigger facing forward, and your right hand which must be straight down by your side, steadying it. On the command to 'shoulder arms,' followed immediately by 'One,' your right hand will lift the rifle upwards with enough force to enable you to let go, thrusting your right hand back down and grasping the neck of the rifle butt. At the same time, your left hand must grasp the front of the rifle at about right shoulder height. You do all that in one movement, smartly on the command. We'll start by all shouting out the command numbers."

"Are you ready, Shoulderrrrr arms, One."

We joined in with the 'One', though not all together, but only half of the men reacted quickly enough to get the rifle generally in the right position. Some were left holding the rifle with both hands on the barrel. Several never moved and six dropped the gun.

"As you were!" came the shout that we were going to get accustomed to in the future. In other words, start again. Half an hour passed before we all ended up correctly in one movement.

"From there, we shout 'Two', immediately transferring the toy with the right hand across to the left shoulder and the left hand taking the weight level with your waist. But your right hand remains on the front of the rifle until the command, 'Three', at which time you bring your right hand back smartly to your side, leaving the rifle, would you believe, on your shoulder."

Human nature decrees that people are different. Some can absorb information quickly and interpret the appropriate actions required. We mortals then have the problem of getting messages from the brain to the limb. Slower learners have the additional headache of having to hurry the next stage, thus leading to inaccurate sequences and failure. Failure was not tolerated by Corporal Preston, who bellowed abuse continuously at the poor wretch who had got it wrong.

"We'll stay out here until you get the message, you ignorant shower. My mother could do better."

"You haven't got a mother," was heard in the ranks. "You were shot up against a wall and hatched in the sun."

Tempers frayed. Corporal Preston demanded to know who had spoken on the parade ground and the mumblings got louder and more personal. Most of us realised that there could be only one winner and kept quiet, anticipating the inevitable. It came in a manner that surprised us all. Sensing that his authority was being challenged, the corporal moved swiftly, bursting into the ranks and cracking two airmen across the knuckles with his cane. Retaliation was equally speedy. One swore unmercifully at the corporal but the other lost his rag entirely and swung his rifle in the direction of the antagonist, causing him to duck instinctively to avoid being beheaded.

"Airmen, attention. Stand easy. You will remain here till I return. AC2 Rogers, accompany me to the guardroom. I'm charging you with attacking a non-commissioned officer. You'll end up in Colchester for this."

We stood around, mentally and physically shattered. Rogers was an idiot although the corporal had continuously made him a scapegoat for the wrong reasons. The colour of Rogers' hair, bright ginger, may have had something to do with it. Rogers stood out in a crowd and as a Scot, he was quick-tempered.

On his return, Corporal Preston had immediate respect from the squad. We had one more go at the drill, which drew comments which were the nearest we ever heard bordering on a compliment from him.

"Right, now that I have only intelligent airmen here, we'll put all that lot together and do the exercise in one continuous movement. But you need a pause between the One, Two, Three so you shout the words 'left, right' in between. The pause will give the sleepy ones a chance to keep up. So, it's 'One, left right, Two, left right, Three' and on 'Three' throw your right arm to your side."

It was a shambles. Four attempts brought little success and with a blasphemous accusation at God for bringing these creatures to him, the corporal muttered "I give up," and dismissed us to our hut with the reminder of the rifle cleaning session to follow after supper. I was certain that secretly, we all shared the same thought, that tonight, there will be no rifle throwing.

During the supper break Rogers' belongings were collected from the hut. We never saw him again and never heard of his plight. Certainly, that episode coloured our thinking for the evening chores which proceeded without mishap. We were introduced to a 'pull-through', which consisted of a piece of string with a metal tag which was fed from the ammunition chamber through the barrel dragging an oily cloth. Unfortunately, they were difficult to handle and took superhuman strength to achieve a result that would please the corporal.

At the end of the session Corporal Preston handed me a letter that he had forgotten to deliver earlier in the day. It brought such enjoyment to my heart that was in dire need of being up-lifted. It ended …

Wednesday 27th April, 1949
…… On reading this letter through, it doesn't seem to say all that my heart says. I find it so difficult to write 'I love you' and make it sound as if it's true. But, believe me darling I DO love you. I could write 'Darling Arthur I love you' all over the page and still mean it. Darling , I miss you so much.

There's an old lady aged 73 years on the wireless singing 'Loves Old Sweet Song'. So you see my darling, love <u>CAN</u> last that long. I know that our love will last much longer.
All my love, always, from your sweetheart,
Ann.

I re-read the letter several times and could imagine my darling Ann actually writing it. I knew how deep her love was, but I needed to be told repeatedly. Probably, that was the reason that I used the same words in my letters to her. All her replies said how much she enjoyed rushing home to read them.

It poured with rain relentlessly throughout the following day, adding to the energy-sapping drill of marching with the rifle. The cold wind numbed our fingers and the rain washed the sweat from our faces. But nobody complained and I could sense the concentration being exerted. Corporal Preston strutted around like a prize cock that had just won a territorial battle with an adversary. His vocabulary expanded and we were likened to mamby–pamby ballet girls, his deaf grandmother and ostriches.

"If you want to be as stubborn as an ostrich, I'll drill you into the ground. Then you can whistle 'The Blacksmith's Blues' until the sparks come out of your arsehole."

By the end of the week we had taken on board the art of marching, changing direction and saluting on the march with the rifle. All we had to do was to co-ordinate our actions together, and that was where we were falling short of the standard. Although he had improved amazingly, Murphy still showed his inability to guarantee a successful execution of any drill programme, but he knew that he had our support and would cover-up for him. He was a very popular member of the team.

The NAAFI on the camp was a popular venue in the evenings. Although food helpings in the dining hall were quite good, the daily exertions usually attracted the need of a light supper. Eggs or beans on toast was a favourite for a shilling, and the tea was always hot. There were two dart boards and a snooker table in a separate room, but we had to hand in our identity cards at the counter for the use of darts and cues. Consequently, nobody ever allowed the tools to be passed to the next players unless the ID had been recovered.

An alternative to the NAFFI was an ASTRA cinema that opened Tuesday and Thursday evenings and weekends. We were like kids at the Saturday morning cinemas back home. Western films were popular, with much jeering and cheering during the performances. It was a way of regaining our sanity, lost during the day's drill.

With no duties over the weekend, several of us decided to spend Saturday afternoon and evening in Liverpool. Jim and I watched Liverpool and Newcastle draw 1-1 in the rain and then gorged ourselves on egg and double chips for two shillings. The evening cost us 9d at a News Theatre where we watched a mass of short cartoon comedies. It was all such a success, that we decided to spend Sunday at New Brighton. A funfair took our fancy, but we were ejected for standing up in the Whips. It was fortunate really, because we had hardly any money to waste.

Spring decided to poke its head from behind the clouds on the Monday, bringing a green woodpecker to the grassed area outside the hut. At least it gave a change in the early morning conversation for several of us, who had begun to forget that there was another world out there. The sunshine brought another surprise in the form of the Sports Officer, who arrived on the parade ground just as we were starting drill.

"Corporal, may I ask you to release the four airmen who volunteered to represent the Wing in the cross-country events. There's a team run in half an hour, meet in the NAAFI. Thank you, Corporal," and he returned Corporal Preston's immaculate salute.

The corporal's language was not as polite as the officer's.

"Let me look at the skiving bastards who think they'll get away with this. You lot couldn't run a tap, let alone five miles. I'll be keeping an eye on you four. Any trouble and you'll be re-flighted."

The run was refreshing, but we learned even better news. We would be in competition with two other teams on Thursday and could go on 48 hour leave on the Friday. I was so excited that I immediately sent a telegram to Ann, telling her the news. Life had taken on a new image. The officer was pleased with our performance and promised two further outings. Each of the passes would include rail vouchers. I couldn't believe my luck. I would soon be with Ann for three consecutive weekends, including 3rd June, Whitsun, which was scheduled to be leading us into our last week of training.

If Corporal Preston was annoyed with my sporting activities, he must have been close to bursting a blood vessel by the end of the week. The officer interviews were gathering pace and I was among twenty from the whole station who had been chosen for the initial talks. Having survived the first three rounds of elimination, I was one of three selected to go to Padgate on the following Monday to face the final panel of top brass. I had cleaned my kit so regularly that I had to buy more Duraglit. Nerves began to take over as I realised that my two opponents had a head start. The favourite for the single spot was an airman whose father was an Air Vice Marshall in London. The other already had passed his Higher Schools Certificate and was awaiting a place at Oxford University. I consoled myself with the thought that perhaps there would be room for two or even three appointments. I entered the interview room, marched smartly to the five officers, saluted and was invited to sit, remove my beret and relax. My expectation of the opening question was correct. All my interviews had been the same.

"Hello, AC2 Allwright, was your journey all right? Ha ha."

All five rocked with laughter at the Wing Commander's wit. It always was a good opening for me because it gave me the opportunity to settle whilst they enjoyed the hilarity. The questioning proceeded for half an hour. No, my father didn't serve in the second war. He was too badly injured at the Somme in the Great War. No, I don't know his rank. No, I have no plans to go to University, I shall be going to a teachers' training college. No, I have no relatives in the RAF. No, I don't live in a detached house, it is a terraced property owned by my parents. I was getting a trifle niggled at the class segregation. Yes, I totally approve of national service and I welcome the opportunity to practice my organising skills. I threw this comment in, as it had been appreciated at the earlier rounds of this project.

"Thank you for attending, airman. We shall be in touch with the recommendations if that is all right with you?" and they all shuffled in amusement.

I had not expected the final joke. I stood, saluted, about turned and went for the door. Horror upon horror, I was carrying my beret which I should have donned before saluting. On my arrival back at West Kirby, a note awaited me. My trip to Padgate had been unsuccessful.

Wednesday 11th May, 1949

My Dearest Ann,
I am sorry to tell you that I have let you and your parents down. I had my final interview for becoming an officer, but failed to pass. I really wanted to show you that I can better myself, but I don't seem to come from the right sort of family. All the questions seemed to be aimed at my dad's status and whether I had any relations who were officers. It hurts all the more because your sister Margaret's boy friend is a Pilot Officer.
Please believe me darling, I shall always try and give you a good life, even though, at present, I have no money to look after you in the manner that you deserve. I was hoping that officer's pay would help us along that road. You are too lovely a lady to let down and I'm so sorry.
Forgive me darling, from your ever-loving husband–to-be,
Arthur.

My disappointment was side-lined on the following morning when more excitement occurred. Lorries took our flight to a nearby firing range for Weapon Training. The idea of crawling through tall grass carrying a rifle didn't appeal to me, especially as we seemed to be sharing the plot with families of frogs. At the end of the trail, there were three exercises firing at targets using our rifle, then pistols and finally, a bren machine gun. My only experience of shooting had been with an air rifle at New Brighton the previous week. I was the laughing stock at the fairground when on-lookers had made ribald comments about the crime of someone like me fighting to save our country.

The advice given to us was that, when in the firing position, the butt of the rifle should be tight against our shoulder, take 'the first pressure' and fire. But each time, I hurt my shoulder with the recoil. Consequently, I failed to obtain the 30% pass mark and together with five other failures, I had to return the next day. The result was worse and the sergeant dived for cover when my bren gun attempt ended with the ammunition hitting the sand just in front of me and describing a gentle arc to the targets and into the sky.

"I'll give you 31% to avoid the risk of you coming back," was his final comment.

On my return to West Kirby, our hut was in turmoil. The 'Station Routine Orders' had just been posted in the NAAFI, showing that our flight would be on duty for the whole of the Whitsun break. We were told by the Bastard that he had arranged it by inviting the Warrant Officer to watch our turn-out on the parade ground recently. He begrudgingly admitted that we could get a 48-hour pass for the coming weekend. This was no consolation for me, because I had now been promised three passes and only two weekends to use them. An added disadvantage was that the Whitsun leave attracted the use of a coach to London which was 12s.6d cheaper than the train which we would have to use.

I was about to post a parcel to Ann, asking her to do some washing for me. It had become a fairly regular practice of mine, starting with collars that needed starching and handkerchiefs and now developing to a couple of shirts. The camp laundry was unreliable and orders got mixed. Already, one of my shirts was a different colour. With my trip home pending, I was able to save the postage.

It was possible that the damp grass at the range took its toll of our men. Three of us ended up in hospital with tonsillitis, necessitating the cancellation of my leave. My main concern was that Ann may be getting fed up with my changing plans. However, she continually reassured me that she understood, but the guilt lay heavily with me in bed. One pleasure that came as a surprise was the wireless in the ward, a luxury that didn't exist in our hut. It was a popular asset, especially on the evening when the British heavyweight boxing title was decided and Bruce Woodcock beat Freddie Mills. The noise was unbecoming in a hospital! The food was exceptionally good and second helpings were commonplace. Otherwise, it was a boring existence. As we progressed to recovery, we were allowed to get up and dress in the hospital uniform of white shirt and red tie. We supposed that this rule acted as a deterrent against trying to escape, as if anyone would want to!

I returned to my flight earlier than expected and my first point of call was to dare to approach the corporal to reassure him that I could retain my position with the team for the passing-out parade due in ten days time. He said that he would let me know. We were suddenly reminded that the cross country matches were imminent with the associated leave passes, but I decided that as the end of my stay at West Kirby was in sight, it would be pointless to put my body through more agony. I informed the sports officer, who readily agreed that he couldn't take the risk of a sick airman collapsing on the course.

There was just the one weekend before the passing–out week and I still had the 48-hour pass from the first cross-country run. With the possibility of having to stay an extra week, I decided to push my luck and go to Admin and get it signed for the Friday. Lady Luck smiled at me and as soon as the morning drill ended, I was away from the camp before the lads returned from their lunch. I was frightened that they may have played pranks to delay me, because of the number of times I had gone home.

The magnetism of love cannot be resisted. Every day of separation seemed to be a wasted day of our lives and even though the weekend was dimmed by the fact that Ann had caught my tonsillitis through the post – how else? Her nearness doubled the value of making the journey.

But my return to the camp on the Sunday at midnight tested my sense of humour. Although it was very dark in the hut I soon realised that my bed had been removed and all the men were asleep or pretended to be. I had two choices and discretion steered me to lie on the floor in my bed space and make the most of it. Fortunately, it was a mild night but I was awake hours before reveille, with every joint reminding me of its presence. I was utterly shattered but happy. Of course, the inmates chuckled relentlessly throughout the day and Corporal Preston, who obviously, had found out why a bed had mysteriously appeared on the parade ground, piled the pressure on me. Being aware of the extent of my absence from camp and determined to ward off any challenge to his authority, he ordered me to do ten minutes drill on my own in front of the flight.

At the end of the session, he called me to the front and to my astonishment, he agreed that I could retain the position of 'right-hand-marker' for the pass-out parade on Wednesday. There was a muffled cheer in the ranks but my 'thank you, corporal,' was met with his regimental sneer and a grunt, which I assumed meant that I had embarrassed him.

The sun got up early on Wednesday, determined to get a good view of the parade. All of the overnight clouds had been dismissed and puddles on the parade ground had disappeared. A gentle breeze from the East tempered the strength of sunrays and conditions were perfect.

The Tuesday evening inspection of our billet and best blue had gone like a dream. But Corporal Preston left nothing to chance. Immediately after breakfast he gave us twenty minutes to prepare for a last-minute parade to 'tone us up', as he called it. He continued to call us all the irreverent names that he could muster, but we were in no mood to react adversely. We possessed a gritty determination to out-perform the other flights, even though it would mean that the Bastard would bathe in the knowledge that he had won. There was no way that we would be beaten. We would march as one. Our timing would be impeccable. Our uniforms' brass would dazzle in the bright sunshine. We were impenetrable. We stamped our immaculately shiny boots onto the metal ground with vicious venom. Even His Majesty would have been proud of this flight, training on his behalf.

We were rewarded with a twenty minute break before the big event was due to start. A pee got priority, then a last minute polish of the brass, with everyone purposely avoiding brushing up against his mates lest he damaged the apparel. Another pee and we were on our own.

The camp band entered the arena, the brass section gleaming in the sun. We had experienced just one rehearsal with music and the grandeur of 'The RAF March Past' stirred the pits of our stomachs. The band's Director marched as though it was his own passing out, when in reality, he was probably sick to death with the number of times that he had performed at these ceremonies. We were called to attention by the Parade Warrant Officer and we were away. Oh the excitement of it all. The adrenalin flowed with the music. The 'eyes right' at the saluting base was sincere. 'About turn' was accomplished as never before. The rifle drill was immaculate. We shouted our timings to ourselves, silently: One, left right, Two, left right, Three, and we thrust our right hand to our sides with an impressive determination. I could sense that we didn't want it to end.

But end, it did. The sun had warmed us to a state of collapse. Sweat poured behind my collar. The Wing Commander announced that all flights had passed and casually left the podium, walking towards us.

"Well done, Corporal," he said, and retired.

We knew that we had been singled out for a dramatic performance. Nobody had come anywhere near us. Corporal Preston retained his composure.

"For the last time, Flight dismissed." And he was gone. No 'well done', no 'thanks', that a more human person would have ventured. Not even a swear word, most unlike the Bastard that we knew. Perhaps that was a compliment.

CHAPTER 3

Jammy and I were friends from the moment that we met at Liverpool Street Station. We had made contact at West Kirby on the evening that the postings had been published and had agreed to travel to Bawdsey together after our week's leave. Having survived our square-bashing in different flights, we had never met previously and as nobody else had selected this Course, I suppose that we were a natural pair. Our travel instructions referred to a bus service from Felixstowe to Old Felixstowe where a ferry would carry us across the River Deben to Bawdsey Manor. Our conversation and jokes during the journey to Ipswich confirmed our compatibility. Both of us had regular girl friends and played cricket. We both enjoyed food in quantity but neither had any money. Jammy lived in Essex and by coincidence, we both hoped to become teachers.

The bus to the ferry turned out to be a figment of the imagination. We would have to wait two and a half hours for the next one.

"We'll have to hoof it," I suggested, not wanting to risk the cost of a taxi. "I'm game if you are."

"It's all very well while we are in the shade," he replied, "but this map shows that the road crosses a golf course. It'll be bloody hot out there."

Our temperaments prevented us from making a decision that would cause conflict, and we just stood there waiting for a brainwave. I then discovered why Jammy got his nick-name. As he was trying to analyse the bus timetable, a haughty, moustached gent driving an old Austin car stopped.

"It's no use reading that, airman. It's last year's. There's a bus on the half hour but I'm going to the golf club so if you can squeeze in I'll take you to the ferry. That's where you're going, isn't it?"

We laughed when we discovered how far away the ferry was. Having passed the clubhouse our host, Jerry, pointed to a small boathouse amidst the few buildings that made up Old Felixstowe.

"Don't ever queue for the boat. Just say 'Air Force' and give him a tanner. Or if you are in uniform, pay tuppence."

We thanked Jerry profusely and he was gone, having done his good deed for the day.

There was no indication where the camp would be in relation to the Manor. As we approached the river, sweating with the weight of kitbags and carrier bags in seventy degrees of summer sun, a swarthy seafaring man, complete with a braided white cap, shouted to us to hurry if we wanted to avoid a two hour dinner break.

"Mr. Brinkley will row you across. Pay him."

From the moment we set foot in his boat, Mr. Brinkley treated us to a Cook's tour of the area. "It is hard to imagine that in 1886, William Cuthbert Quilter, the local MP woke up one morning and decided to build Bawdsey Manor on the land over there. Land that he had purchased at auction.

"The site is at the end of a peninsula with a beautiful sandy beach bordering the North Sea and separated from Old Felixstowe by this river. Unless you want a forty mile detour via Woodbridge, you'm have to take the ferry. My family have operated this for three generations. My father, Charles Brinkley, had a hook instead of his left hand but still managed to row against the tide. You'll be forbidden to enter the water here because of the force of the tide. You wouldn't be the first, or the twenty-first body to be swept out to sea."

"OK," I thought, "so you've earned your tuppence to get me across."

"Quilter must have been a perfectionist. Took eighteen years and five attempts to achieve what it is today. The Manor remained the family home until 1936 when, together with 168 acres of land and outbuildings, it was purchased by the Air Ministry for £24,000."

Brinkley aimed the boat upstream, rowing strongly to counteract the tide that swirled around us.

"The Manor was bought to allow Sir Robert Watson-Watt to develop radar and those pylons were erected as part of a chain of radar stations along the South and East coasts giving early warning of the approach of enemy aircraft during the Second World War. Jerry tried to bomb them but we got away with it. You'll be radar trainees, I suppose?"

It was a throw-away question that didn't demand, or receive, an answer. Both Jammy and I knew that we were here to learn about radar but we would show only ignorance if we got involved in a conversation on the subject. I was more concerned that the boat seemed to be missing the jetty on the Manor side of the river, by a considerable amount. I gripped the boat nervously. I saw no attraction in being swept out to sea. It was already approaching the specified latest time for us to report at the camp and the last thing I wanted was to be branded a trouble maker at a new station.

My fears were unfounded, however, and as we clunked against the landing stage an RAF corporal, without jacket or cap, welcomed us to Bawdsey and grabbed my kitbag, which he balanced on his shoulder. He waved at us to follow him onto the site and into a rather ornate guardroom.

"You can take your eyes off the Manor, that's for officers and senior ranks. Your billets are over there amongst the trees. They're quite good, really."

The Corporal checked our 1250 identity cards and pointed to a pile of bed linen.

"Two sheets and two pillow cases. Choose any unclaimed beds in Blocks One, Two or Three and they're yours for the duration. You'll enjoy it here. Tea is from five thirty in the Manor Annexe."

Jammy and I looked at each other in disbelief. Surely we had come to the wrong place? The Manor reminded me of Hampton Court Palace, the gardens of which were a favourite haunt for Ann and me on our cycling trips. I had never been in a hotel in my life and here I was, living in a place like this. Even more unbelievable was the reception at the ferry. Corporals aren't supposed to be nice blokes.

The blocks each housed six beds and there were two empty beds in Block Three. The other four beds had been taken by airmen from Padgate who had already made-up their beds and unpacked. There was a buzz of excitement in the room as we exchanged experiences of our square-bashing and the unexpected reception at Bawdsey. We all retained the nick-names from the previous camps, mine being "Lefty" and seemed to hit it off from the start. The other four left to explore the site, but Jammy and I had a similar alternative priority, that of writing to our girlfriends to send our new address.

I wrote in a happy vein :

23rd June, 1949

Well, Darling, I have arrived at the new "camp." I wouldn't call it a camp because all it consists of is a large Manor House, just like our Hampton Court, and a few annexes for our school, the NAAFI and our living blocks. I cannot believe my luck. If only I could stay here for the whole eighteen months. I'm told that there is a lovely sandy beach behind the camp, but I haven't seen it yet. If only you could be here with me. It would be even better than the time that I spent with you and your mum and dad last week in Llandudno. I was so unhappy leaving you yesterday, to come here, but the look of the place has cheered me up.

This is just a quick note to give you my address. As long as you put 'Course 91, 5 RS', RAF Bawdsey, Suffolk, it will find me Ok. ………
From your loving husband-to-be,
Arthur."

I put a tuppence halfpenny stamp on the envelope and Jammy offered to run to the admin block to catch the evening post.

This left me alone to reminisce on the week that I had just spent with Ann. Her mum and dad had written secretly to Mrs. Roberts, in whose guest house they were booked for a two week holiday, asking her to allow me to join them for the first week. So when I had arrived home for my week's leave from West Kirby, I had just enough time to say 'Hello'
to my mum and dad before packing to join Ann's family on the train to North Wales.

We had enjoyed a week of romantic adventure and on several occasions Ann's parents had allowed us to go out alone. We walked for miles, hand in hand, talking of the far-off time when we could get married. On one occasion on the beach with her parents, Ann actually changed into a swimming costume. It was the first time that I had seen her in it and I was extremely embarrassed as I tried not to watch her mother holding a large towel round her as Ann changed. In return I caused much hilarity by producing a pair of RAF shorts that were slightly too big for me. I always enjoyed making Ann's dad laugh. Being a heavy smoker he had mastered the art of laughing or talking with a cigarette wedged in the corner of his mouth. He had his own cigarette machine, using Old Gold tobacco, so the fags were usually very thin.

"It's my way of cutting down," he used to say.

My reminiscing was interrupted by the return of Jammy, shouting that the rest of the gang were already in the canteen. We rushed to the Manor, not knowing what to expect. The canteen was 'the dining room' and instead of queuing with about fifty others, all pushing and shoving, as had been the case at West Kirby, the choices of food were discreetly set out at an attractive hatchway inviting two queues, each with only half a dozen people. There were two choices of main course and a pudding. Instead of doorsteps of bread, medium slices were on offer, which meant that I took twice as many pieces than I would have taken at West Kirby. The canteen staff was a mix of airmen and WRAFS, which explained the nicety of having a small bottle of flowers on each table. There was a sink in the corner allowing us to wash our 'irons' before leaving the room.

Our evening exploration led us to the NAAFI, the Deben Club, which was one of the few places where non-commissioned officers, WRAFS and airmen mixed, to drink, play darts, billiards or cards, or eat snacks. It was the shop for our home comforts, toiletries, sweets, writing paper and library books. One of the Manor rooms had become the cinema, seating about fifty, and was open to all ranks.

The mood in our billet at ten thirty was jovial. None of us had expected what we had experienced and the tiredness brought about by travelling and settling in, contributed to my ability to overcome the noise of the creaking springs of my iron bedstead, and I slept soundly.

Our course opening day commenced with a tour of the site. It was confirmed that officers and senior ranks slept in the Manor, whilst WRAFS had quarters nearby. A thick white line showed the demarcation between the sexes and anybody found on the wrong side would be disciplined. Some of us accepted it as a good thing, knowing that we had no intention of mixing with the girls. One or two, however, laughed and saw it as a challenge.

The Manor was a beautifully ornate building with fairytale towers. Wooden wall panels, grand stairways and comfortable common rooms graced the inside. One large lounge area had been allocated for anybody to use as a reading room and Jammy nudged me, indicating that this would suit us for our letter writing. Another room, probably one of the banqueting halls, was the cinema and films were advertised for the following Wednesday and Saturday. A notice headed 'Dress', told us that personnel could wear civilian dress in the Manor. Our course tutor nodded.

"Yes, you can wear civvies at any time when you're not on duty; that includes going into Old Felixstowe. It's best blue, though, when you go on leave. And talking of leave, the course lasts for five weeks, that's four weekends, but you will get only one 48 hour pass; the rest can be only 36 hours. So, Course 91, that's you, will have a coach laid on for the weekend after next, July1st".

"Blimey," I said out loud, "that means we can't get our civvies for two weeks."

The tour ended at the school and we were introduced to the Head Tutor, a WRAF sergeant. This station never ceased to spring surprises and this was yet another one. The strange thing was that she commanded silence immediately for two reasons. Firstly, her sense of humour, and secondly she had firm breasts that were bursting to check the weather. A piece of paper dropped onto my lap.

'Ten shillings for the first airman to prove whether or not they're real.'

The sniggering caught her attention.

"Ok," she called, "what's it all about?" And after a second or two, she looked down to see that a blouse button had blown its base and without hesitation, she lifted her bosoms, one in each hand, as if to make them comfortable and demonstrating at the same time that they were 'all hers'.

"Now that we have sorted out that little boys' craving, let's get on with our work."

There was a strange pong in the billet on the second morning. We had finished 'ablutions' and were about to wander over for breakfast. Laughter at the far end of the room broadcast the news that the aroma was some posh-smelling stuff used by Brian. He was immediately dubbed with the name 'Lavender'.

"Fancy having to live with a name like that," giggled Jammy. "It's his own fault, I suppose, for wanting to smell like a tart."

The teasing went on all through breakfast and into the lecture room where the WRAF sergeant picked on him continuously for answers. A friendly atmosphere had developed between us and the tutors. We were beginning to realise that the aggression at the square-bashing had not followed us to Bawdsey. The discipline regarding dress, punctuality and general behaviour remained and was respected, but we felt like human beings again.

The big surprise on the third day was the revelation that much of the information regarding radar that we were being taught was virtually out-of-date. Some of the notes given to us had been extracted from Sir Watson-Watt's own papers prepared during the development stages between 1936 and 1940.

"Your exams at the end of the Course will be based on what we've given you, but the systems used at your next postings will vary from site to site. So you'll get up-to-date 'gen' when you arrive."

The general principles showed that Watson-Watt was obviously a brilliant man and the country owed a lot to him for his contribution to the outcome of the war. By sending out signals which picked up approaching aircraft, radar operators could monitor the reflected responses, thus detecting height, speed and direction of the machines. The information could then be relayed to personnel in an operations room, who would have direct contact with the RAF's intercepting planes. Modern sophistication centred on the speed at which information could be gathered and acted upon.

Away from the lecture room, I had other priorities, in particular those relating to the acquisition of a signed 36 hour pass for the weekend ahead. The earliest that I would be allowed to leave camp would be 0800 on Saturday, so train times would be all-important to maximise my time at home. As Ann would not be returning from Llandudno until late Saturday, I could expect to see her for only a few hours on Sunday. However, this would give me time to sort out some civvies to take back to Bawdsey. I had no idea from where I could borrow a case.

I was so excited as I walked to see her and hoped that she would agree to walking to Cannon Hill Common for the afternoon. But Ann had other plans. Her hair needed washing and her mother would not allow her out until it had dried. I got cross, called her selfish and when we parted for my return to camp, I refused to kiss her. Now, I needed to clear the air urgently, in time for the long weekend pass already approved for the following Friday. I wrote …

4th July, 1949.

My Darling,
I really can't say "Sorry", enough, for my behaviour yesterday. I suppose that I looked forward so much to be alone with you and go for a walk somewhere, that I didn't stop to think of your need to get over your holiday. I saw that the sun had made your hair shine so I was mean to ignore your own wishes to wash it, ready for work.
I think that your mum noticed that we had argued so I hope you can tell her that I'm sorry. They were so good to have me on holiday with them ………
From your husband- to-be,
Arthur.

I felt better as soon as I had posted the letter; so much so, that I found myself volunteering to do gardening work during our free time on the Monday afternoon. I hadn't realised that the 'work' was watering the cricket pitch. This, in turn, led me to meeting two of the officers and a flight sergeant, who were marking out a wicket and boundaries for the Wednesday match, Resident Staff v Trainees. A bonus of automatic selection was the reward for working on the pitch. The prospect of playing on such a good wicket took over my mind, but I was brought down to earth when a letter arrived from Ann.

4th July, 1949

My Dearest Arthur,
I was so unhappy after you had argued last night. I couldn't sleep and I can't believe that you meant all those horrible things. I think mum is very cross but she hasn't said anything. She likes you very much but wouldn't want to hear all that you said. I love you so much. I hope you will be in a better mood next weekend.
Something else that I didn't tell you yesterday; I have been invited to Derek L's 18th birthday party tomorrow. I hope that you won't be cross about that. I promise I'll be good. I won't enjoy myself half as much because you won't be there with me. Please believe me darling. Shall I tell Derek that you will be available for cricket on Sunday for the youth club? ....
From your wife-to-be,
Ann.

6th July, 1949

My Darling Ann,
Your letter has made me even more unhappy. I cannot forgive myself for being so mean, especially after such a good time away with you. I meant everything I said on holiday about looking forward to being your husband, to look after you for ever.
Of course I don't mind you going to the party. I really hope that you have a good time. And yes, please get me a game for Sunday, unless you would prefer to do something else.

From your husband- to- be,
Arthur.

My mixed-up feelings about Ann's letter and the embarrassment of the next meeting with Ann's parents, conflicted with the work at Bawdsey and the impending cricket match. I lay awake for several hours and my thoughts kept returning to the party that Ann was enjoying at that very moment. There would probably be kissing games and although she assured me that I needn't worry, that was exactly what I was doing. I would have to be very careful at the weekend.

Wednesday afternoon arrived in a blaze of sunshine. But that turned out to be the only 'bright' thing about it. The Staff team were all properly kitted–out in whites, and two of the officers had actually played for Cheshire. In contrast, none of our team had whites and only two of us wore plimsolls. The rest had no choice but to wear their black working boots.

The next shock was that I was told to open the bowling as a fast bowler, something that I had never done. The most accurate description of my bowling was 'right arm optimistic'. But with the aid of two boundary catches and a dubious lbw decision, I ended up with five wickets for twenty-four runs and the Staff were all out for seventy-eight runs. Our quality was reflected in a dismal dismissal for eight runs, two of which were extras for wides.

The weekend passed off pleasantly. My stubbornness was not mentioned and Ann's mum gave me a case for my civvies. The weather was abysmal but as the cricket was a non-event, Ann and I sat for several hours in the 'Best Room' playing some of her dad's gramophone records. There seemed to be a bit of competition with next door, because Mr. Diamond was playing his favourite piano rendering of "Scherzo" and the thin walls allowed us to marvel at the number of notes that Chopin hadn't even thought of including in his Nocturne Opus 9 No. 2. Ann's dad often made us laugh when we heard Mr. Dimond starting up.

"And now we have yet another version of that famous Italian Joker Op 9, Mark 293"

Ann's mum gave us tea on our own, but we all forgot to keep an eye on the clock, resulting in me rushing to London and missing my train. The only remaining train arrived in Ipswich too late to catch a connection to Felixstowe and it was then that I met two other defaulters wondering what to do. None of us had enough money for a taxi so we decided to walk the sixteen miles to the ferry. At the halfway stage we celebrated by sitting in the middle of the road and peeling two oranges. Having left the peel neatly spelling the words '8 to go', we eventually arrived at the ferry at 5am, much too early for the first crossing. I was completely shattered.

Our bravado got the better of us and ignoring the camp orders regarding unsupervised river activities, we searched for a likely craft to 'borrow'. Fortunately, we were being watched and a friendly fisherman took pity on us and rowed us over. He was happy enough to accept twenty Players Weights cigarettes for his trouble. The snores in the guardroom were the only sounds of life and we gratefully crept to our billets for a snatch of sleep.

11th July, 1949

My Dearest, Darling Ann,
Although I wrote to you this morning, I am so happy that I must write and tell you how much you mean to me. Jammy is with me and we are perched on a cliff ledge about seventy feet above the beach on a lovely sunny evening. Both of us are writing to our special darlings.
All the rest of the courses are at the camp dance in the Manor, but neither of us wanted to mix with other girls. I know that Jammy thinks the world of his Brenda, but he cannot love her as I love you, for the simple reason that real love can only come to people who understand and plan for each other as we do.
I'm glad that Jammy is my friend because we are similar in nature. That's why we are together here at this moment. The others are probably enjoying themselves but it's not our idea of fun. We both want to be true to our darling wives to be.
There is just no girl in the whole world who is half as kind, beautiful and generous as you, sweet Ann.
It is so lovely sitting here listening to the waves smashing against the wall, reminding me of our lovely week in Llandudno. Fifteen months to go and then we really can start our years of companionship. ....
From your ever-loving husband–to-be
Arthur.

13th July, 1949

My Extra-special Darling, ...
Yesterday was the first day that I've missed writing to you and I'm very sorry. I started one in the evening but suddenly remembered that I had to press my tunic and Best Blue, ready for the weekend.

Do you want a laugh ? I have been made a Course Leader, probably for all the crawling that I do to get weekend passes. The only advantage is that I wear a lanyard on my shoulder and this allows me to jump the queues in the dining room and NAAFI. Each morning I have to parade our Course 91. But next week we shall be the Senior Course and I'll have to parade the whole school at the final get-together. Can you imagine anybody listening to me? Every time, so far, the blokes have taken the mickey and it's been one long laugh. Jammy is the worst at making me bust with laughter as we march to the school.

One bit of bad news. We won't be getting paid before the weekend, so I won't be able to pay you the ten shillings that you spent on your sister Margaret's present.

The food here is still great. Breakfast we had corn flakes, bacon, fried spuds, sausage and bread. For dinner, there was liver, thick gravy, spuds and greens, followed by rhubarb and custard. For tea we had spuds, lettuce, meat loaf, toms, beetroot, hard-boiled egg, bread, butter and peach jam. Not bad for a day's food eh?

Good-night my darling angel.

From your husband-to-be, ...

Arthur.

The final week became a challenge, not to be the only one to fail the exams. Jammy and I put in an extra two evenings work practising plotting on the ops table and we became quite proficient at it. Everybody found the visual display board the hardest to operate. We had to stand behind the huge opaque panel and write back-to-front and from right to left. This enabled the officers in the ops room, on the other side of the screen, to act on the information that we were producing.

The examinations were unexpectedly serious and were administered in a strict fashion. The written work was followed by each individual's practical plotting technique and when we thought that it was all over, we were invited, one by one to an oral interview. The crafty tutors had kept this a secret.

Fortunately, the RAF Stations awaiting new personnel must surely have been desperate, because the whole course was passed with no marks lower than 80%. With the announcement of the results, we were told of our postings. Unfortunately, Jammy and I would be parting company. He accepted Neatishead in Norfolk whilst I would be searching the map for a little village called Sandwich, in Kent.

Sad Friday arrived. It was good-bye Jammy and thanks for his fun and companionship. Good-bye to the Manor, the two pubs of Old Felixstowe, The Victoria and The Ferry Boat Inn. A final good-bye hug from Betty the WRAF tutor. As Mr. Brinkley rowed me across the Deben for the last time, I looked back at the remote Manor building that still retained so many secrets about radar, Sir Watson-Watt and the war. Surely the phrase 'Events that changed the tide of the war ….' must have had some connection with the magical developments that were hatched in that place, beside the fast-flowing river. I left Old Felixstowe, confident that my experiences at Padgate, West Kirby and now, Bawdsey, meant that the worst was over, and that I was equipped with an understanding that it was not immoral to be a crawler with authority. The eighteen months national service was a mandatory penance. Maximising the time that I could spend with my darling Ann was still a greater challenge.

CHAPTER 4

21st July, 1949

My Own Dearest Ann,
Thank you so much for bothering to meet Derek and me as we passed through London yesterday evening. Derek was most impressed with you and it showed how much you love me. You really are a darling.
Our train didn't arrive in Sandwich until 11.30pm and we were lucky to be on it! It was only because the guard came to our carriage at Ashford to tell us that we should be in the front of the train. Our carriage would have taken us to Margate. He came again at Sandwich to find us both asleep.
The streets were very dark, with no lighting. Three people gave us directions but we still got lost. Eventually we found Stonar House which used to be a girls school and we were shown to our room. Luckily, we are sharing a two-man billet.
I'll write again later today, when I've settled down. I love you so much. The first thing I shall do today will be to see how often I can expect to get home to see you darling.
From your husband to be,
Arthur.

Several shocks awaited us on our first live day at Sandwich. A loud banging on our door at 8.30am brought us to our senses. Someone was trying to open the locked door.

"If there's anyone in there, I want to know why. Outside on fatigue parade at 9am."

I sat bolt upright in bed. Derek was unmoved by the commotion. He was lying outside the bedclothes, his navy shorts concealing his staff that was urging release. Unperturbed, he grunted, and realised that deflation was required and drew his knees to his chin, and farted.

"Sorry about that, Arthur. Must have been dreaming, if only !"

He sat on the edge of his bed, yawning and scratching his balls.

"I vote we take no notice of that prat. Last night the AC1 in the guardroom mentioned something about going to admin this morning to get the gen. Let's find the breakfast, then wash. We can sort out the minor things later. Wasn't it hot in the night?"

I was beginning to warm to Derek. He seemed to get his priorities right and not to be disturbed by diversions. Although we had known each other for only four days, we had already earmarked several areas of similar likes and dislikes. A stock of spare food for eating in the billet was high on the list. We both thought that keeping a low profile for a few days was essential, while we ascertained who could benefit us most in our endeavours to get weekend passes.

As we emerged from our room, we discovered that we had a downstairs room in a two- storey quadrangle. Although the upstairs walkway outside the rooms was made of wooden slats, the noise was minimal. We were to discover later that some airmen had been on duty during the night and waking them early would not be advisable. Several were notorious for having short fuses. It was obvious that this was a small RAF station, housing a maximum of 150 men. Officers lived with their families off-site, mainly in Ramsgate and surrounding areas. Duty officers had quarters on site but away from other ranks.

There was only a handful of men at breakfast, the hungry ones. Apparently, when there had been a night 'watch', it was customary for the following day's practice to be cancelled and breakfast would often be sacrificed for a lie-in.

Ian Greenwood, one of two station telephone operators, stood with us at the serving hatch awaiting his fry-up. His battle dress top and trousers, being extremely faded, gave us the impression that Ian was an old hand in the service.

"Sit with me over by the window and I'll fill you in with all the secrets".

He added four thick slices of pretend toast to his breakfast handed to him by an immaculately attired chef, Graham. The overloaded plate of two eggs, four sausages and fried potatoes made it difficult for Ian to balance his mug of thick brown tea, but he managed to negotiate the journey safely.

"You're both new aren't you?" Graham was quick to realise that he had never seen us.

"The ration is one sausage, one egg and as much potato and bread as you wish. It no use looking over at 'Gossip Greenwood', we have an arrangement. He operates the telephone exchange and controls the number of telephone calls that I can have".

Our briefing from Gossip left us bemused. As Fighter Plotters, we were not supposed to be at Sandwich. The filter room in which our duties would have been carried out had suffered a serious fire and a replacement room was unlikely to be commissioned for at least three months. Consequently, we would be acting as radar operators, watching the movement of aircraft and reporting to officers who controlled any necessary interceptions. Those 'watches' were scheduled for Monday, Tuesday and Friday mornings and Thursday and Saturday afternoons. Night watches from 9.30pm to 1am occurred three times per week. During the night watches, pairs of planes would be 'scrambled' from various local airfields and come under the control of our officers who would practice interceptions, using our radar equipment, so the accuracy of the information fed to the officers by the radar operators was paramount.

There was a flag-raising 'fatigue parade' at 8am every morning, at which Sgt Platt, the disciplinary non-commissioned officer, allocated jobs for everyone who couldn't think of a reason for escaping his clutches i.e. sickness, or pending watches. He had heard all the likely far-fetched stories for not being available and only the 'clever buggers', as he called them, were able to side-step him.

We learnt that Stonar House was only the living quarters and the worksite was on the other side of the adjacent toll bridge over the River Stour and about a mile up the Ash Road.

Derek's plan to let Admin sort us out paid off. As relative newcomers to the service, we trod carefully, allowing the permanent staff to do all the talking, but letting it be known that we were keen to use weekend leave passes as often as possible.

"Ah, you love birds, I see, frightened that the missus will be legging over the lodger. Let 'em do it if it keeps them happy. Plenty round here for you if you're prepared to go to Ramsgate or Deal." Then, after a pause whilst the clerk shared a lewd aside with a corporal, he added, "there's a pile of blank passes on this desk. Get one initialled by your duty orderly confirming that you're not listed for watches, and get it in here by Tuesday noon each week for leave on the following Friday. You cannot pick up the signed pass before 12 noon Friday and don't forget to ask for a ration card or your mummy will be cross. Oh, by the way. You can get a travel warrant once a month."

Nothing else mattered. We had got the information we wanted. All we had to do was to find out how watches were allocated and keep our fingers crossed. Our first encounter with fellow fighter plotters was in the NAAFI after lunch and their main interest related to our experiences at West Kirby. Corporal Preston certainly had made his mark on everyone who had met him. But apparently his groups were always praised for their pass-out parades. Everybody hated the man, but being out of his reach enabled us to joke about the experience. On the question of work allocation, we soon got the news that we wanted to hear.

"The airmen fall into two categories. The Scots, Northerners and those who don't want to go home at weekends stay on camp. But as it so boring, they volunteer for the weekend watches, guard duties and Fire Pickets. The others do most of the night watches. Just let it be known which group you're in"

We were then directed to the NAAFI notice board that displayed all the duty rotas and neither of our names appeared after Friday morning, although I was due to do Fire Picket on Monday at 1pm. Fortunately, I would be taking over from Dave who was showing us the board and he quickly put my mind at rest, saying that if my return train was late he would stay until I reported back. This proved to be the start of a great friendship between us.

The weekend however, did not match the enthusiasm with which I had approached it. The train times displayed in the NAAFI were illusions of a make-believe world. Ann had waited at London Bridge for two hours after the scheduled arrival time on the Friday evening, before deciding to go home. Eventually, I called at her house at 10.30pm to find that she had gone to bed, thus denying me of a much-longed-for kiss and cuddle. Her dentist appointment on Saturday prevented our meeting until the afternoon, by which time she was sore. To add to my misery, I had cancelled my planned cricket match for the Sunday in favour of a walk to Cannon Hill Common with Ann, but all we did was to row over silly things.

My return train on the Monday was equally late but Dave was true to his word and I relieved him at 3pm. Two hours late. My brain pounded in sympathy with my hurting heart. Why had I been so foolish with Ann? It was she who deserved attention, not the hard-done me. My pen wrote with passion, reflecting the remorse in my heart.

27th July, 1949

My own dear darling Ann,
What can I say about the weekend? I know I promised not to mention it any more, but I can't sleep or think properly until I've done my best to let you know how sorry in my heart, I really am. You, (who has been so sweet as to be able to love me, still, after the vile things I said to you), deserve nothing but the dearest attention and love from me. I have no right to harbour anything but the sincere thanks for the kindness and unselfish thoughts that you express to me.

Please forgive me again for my jealous thoughts and let me prove to you that my heart and life will always be for you. I adore you.

With all my Love always. Your Husband –to-be,
Arthur

I immediately felt better for being able to express my true feelings but I wouldn't be certain that Ann had really forgiven me until our next meeting in two weeks time. I made up my mind to bombard her with loving letters which truly reflected my love for her. I knew inside me that we would be together for ever, but the occasional thoughts of her being so far away, with nothing but homely things to occupy her time, allowed my more sinister thoughts of losing her, surface.

27th July, 1949
Dear Darling Ann,
I am on duty at the Operations Site and will be here until 1am. It's not all bad news because in the tea breaks I shall be able to write to you. I have just been tracking the course of an aircraft over South West London. The pilot didn't know how lucky he was, to be so close to you, darling. If only I could have been with him so that I could look down and know that you were safely asleep, dreaming of us being together. I shall never be really happy until we are dreaming as one.

28th July, 1949

My Darling,
I have no news but I just want to tell you how much you mean to me. I know that you feel the same. The way you look into my eyes thrills me and if a tiny thing like that is so pleasing, then we must be the most suited couple ever to love one another. I cannot wait for our next

weekend together to arrive. Yes please, I would like to go with you to the art exhibition. There will be plenty of time to get to Wimbledon speedway after.

I'm planning to cycle back to camp on the following Monday, as you suggested, so I'll have to put the alarm clock on for 5am and hope that I can make it. From your ever-loving husband-to-be,
Arthur.

28th July, 1949

My Dear Darling Arthur,
I had two letters waiting for me tonight. You really are sweet to write so much. I love you with all my heart and always will. Although my pen keeps running out of ink, I've just written six pages to sister Margaret who is on holiday. So I'll have writer's cramp by the time this letter is finished. Although my writing is getting fainter, my love for you isn't. All my Love, Always, Ann.

They say that time heals everything and once again time was on my side. Our deep love for each other seemed to overcome all my tantrums which were based, I must admit, on my jealous streak that kept raising its head. Two consecutive weekends of happiness however, repaired the previous damage and Ann's brilliant idea about the bike being so useful around the camp, showed me that she loved me enough to worry about those little niceties. It would halve the travelling time to the tech site, allowing me to have ten minutes extra in bed each morning.

The alarm clock shattered my dreams at the unearthly hour of 4.30am on the Monday chosen for the adventure of cycling to camp. But it was pouring with rain so Plan B kicked in and I made a dash to catch the first train to London to meet the Sandwich connection. That arrangement made me cross because each journey cost me eleven shillings and threepence and I was short of money. I had already borrowed ten shillings from Ann on the previous weekend and pay-day was two weeks away.

The weather was kinder on the following Monday and I began my tortuous journey via Croydon, Bromley, Swanley, and Dartford, where I joined the A2 main road which I hoped would take me to Ramsgate. Cycling in my uniform, including ordinary shoes was extremely tiring and I was shattered by the time I reached Rochester, but lady luck paid me a call which changed my lifestyle for several months.

My tired legs forced me to stop in a roadside café where I got into conversation with a driver.

"Good job the Air Force had planes in the war. We'd never have beaten Jerry on bikes" and the other customers laughed.

"Where are you making for?"

"Sandwich by midday, or I'm on a charge".

"Sandwich? Bloody Hell. You're in luck. Just say the word and you'll be there in an hour".

"One word? I'll say five. Yes please, thanks very much".

Outside in the car park we made for a yellow and white van, marked with the Company logo, 'Achille Serre'.

Give me a minute to move some of the stuff. It's full of clean laundry. We don't want to get your oil on it".

As we sped along the A2 the news got better and better. Jim made the trip from London to Sandwich every Monday. He suggested that if I could get to a spot on that road, he would be only too pleased to give me a lift to camp.

"Falconwood station is your place. Get a train from London Bridge. I pass by at 10am. If you're not there at the side of the road I won't wait, 'cos I have a full day of deliveries. It won't matter if you're not at home for the weekend, then nobody has to worry. If you're at Falconwood there's a free ride for you".

By the time we got to Sandwich my head was spinning. Derek was equally intrigued with the possibilities. What if Jim would bring both of us? He could get from Essex to London and out to Falconwood just as easily as me. I said that I would try and fix it next week. In the meantime, the thought of saving money triggered a more ambitious plan. I had seen several airmen standing outside the camp in the evenings, hitching lifts into Ramsgate. Why not hitch-hike to London on a Friday afternoon?

CHAPTER 5

8th August, 1949

My own dearest darling Ann,
Please excuse the unromantic paper, but I'm on Fire Piquet at the moment and it is the only paper that I can find. I've just had the best supper, ever. You see, the piquet office is just behind the Officers' quarters and a batman for the CO has brought me some left-overs. Two hard-boiled eggs, lettuce, cold spud, tomato, salad cream and 4 slices of the tastiest beef I've ever had. I had to look twice, but it went down very well.

I wish that I could have shared it with you because I could not have afforded it when we go out. You are so kind to put up with me when you could so easily go and enjoy yourself with somebody who could afford more expensive outings, while I'm away. But you are so true and lovely.

I must go and wake up the chap who will take over from me at midnight. Then I can get some sleep and dream of you and the lovely times that we have had.
From your ever-loving husband to be,
  Arthur.

The problems with having no money were never very far from me. But the hitch-hiking on Fridays had certainly stopped me from having to borrow from Ann at the weekends. She had a couture dressmaking job for a very expensive fashion house in Stratford Place, a tiny cul-de-sac off Oxford Street. But the 'rag trade' was noted for the sweat–shop approach to employment and Ann's wages were a pittance compared with the quality input brought about by her trade training. Discipline, especially with regard to timekeeping, was notoriously severe at her workplace and one minute's late arrival at her machine would attract a fifteen minute deduction from the wage packet. Consequently, the girls responded by sitting in a downstairs ABC café for fifteen minutes if they were on the verge of being late for work.

My target each Friday was to try and get to Stratford Place in time to meet Ann as she left work. She appeared to enjoy showing me off to her workmates even though my nature was to be relatively shy in other girls' company. But my uniform tended to give me a boost, hiding the embarrassment.

10th August, 1949

My own darling Arthur,
Thank you for your very sweet letter. You really are a darling. To return your compliment, you are true to me and don't go out from camp spending money. Although I must tell you that I've just been out with Pam, from work, this evening. What do you think of that? We went swimming in the baths behind Liberty's in Regent Street. We had a jolly good laugh and afterwards, went to Fortes for a snack and the whole evening cost only 1s 4d.
My sister Margaret's boy friend John came visiting last night, showing off his RAF officer's uniform. I didn't like to tell him that you look much smarter in your uniform, because he is a bit thin and his jacket just hangs on him. You fill yours! And I'm proud to walk out with you.
I am so much in love with you. I hope that you manage to get home on Friday, especially if you are standing there when I get out of work. My heart will be pounding .
All my love,
 Ann.

The night flights were cancelled on the Thursday and Derek and I decided to indulge in a bit of culture. A local historian had offered to give a talk in the NAAFI on the history of Sandwich. We learnt that Sandwich had been very prosperous in the Middle Ages.

In early times, the fishing fleets maintained by the South East coastal towns, were pressed frequently into service to convey people and armies to and from the continent, as well as to fight battles at sea. They formed the first navy, and in return for the use of their vessels the ports received privileges from the Crown.

Gradually, the ports grouped together and during the reign of Edward The Confessor, the five main harbours of Sandwich, Dover, Hythe, Romney and Hastings became The Cinque Ports. But the navy had long gone and the little village of Sandwich had been taken over by the RAF and I was part of that changing history.

The middle of August gave us a taste of what happens in a heat wave. Stonar House had the problem of an enclosed courtyard, preventing any breeze from infiltrating the living quarters. Derek and I tried sleeping with the billet door and window open. But this was not a good idea. At 2am on the first night of the heat wave, I became aware of a scratching noise that started getting on my nerves. Imagine the shock when I switched on my torch, with the beam shining straight into the eyes of a huge rat. It was more like a rabbit. In fact I wished that it had been a rabbit. My frightened yell brought a rasping rebuke from Derek who thought that I was having a nightmare. He soon shared my concern but even by closing the door, neither of us was sure that another rat wasn't hiding under the bed.

The tech site had a greater problem caused by the lack of any air conditioning. The radar screens gave off heat naturally, but the additional humidity made it necessary to restrict working on the apparatus to half hour stints.

The heat even got to the toll bridge. One afternoon we were delayed for two hours at the bridge on our return from work. We saw a 200-ton coaster pass through but the girders had expanded and there was an 18 inch gap preventing the bridge from closing. The coaster, which had already moored, made fast a towing rope to the bridge and pulled, but without success. People on both sides of the toll were calling out their diverse and interesting solutions and the humour seemed to calm the few irate drivers. Naturally, it was no joke for 'Grumpy', one of our over-weight career airmen at Stonar, whose concern was that our dinner would be ruined. But even he laughed when we offered him to the bridge maintenance unit as human ballast. Eventually, however, a jack was brought into service and this did the trick by closing the gap, just as the jack broke.

Somebody with a sense of humour decided to arrange a rugby match against RAF Manston during the heat wave. I was chosen to add weight to the scrum. Actually I had volunteered to play, saying that I had played regularly for my school, Mitcham County and the Old Mitchamians. I heard that the team would be in line for several days' leave for representing the camp, so there could have been an ulterior motive. On our arrival at Manston we realised that the opposition was fielding a team containing three county players. We lost 8 – 5 with the winning try being scored just as a plane took off, roaring inches above our heads and making us fall flat on our faces. It was the first plane I had seen since joining the Air Force. Most of us suffered cut knees because the field resembled tar macadam, but it was a small price to pay or the scrumptious meal that followed.

The promise of leave was honoured and I plucked up courage to ask Ann if she would like to go to Blagdon, where I had been evacuated during the war, and spend a weekend with 'Auntie' Floss, Gervase and Margaret. At the same time, I wrote to Blagdon. For the next three days I watched anxiously for the post and both replies came on the same day, agreeing to the proposal. My excitement boiled over and Derek came to my rescue when he realised that I had forgotten an extra guard duty and turned up for me. But my planning bore fruit and I started my week's leave on the following Friday, armed with a travel warrant to Bristol and ration cards for two, one of which I had to buy from an admin guy for twenty cigarettes.

The weekend was a great success, with Auntie re-living many of our wartime experiences, but on our return home I had three days leave at my own home while Ann went to work. My mother commented that I was like a fish out of water without my girl friend. My two younger sisters were still at school and the eldest sister worked in a Co-op shop in Raynes Park, in the cash office. Co-op customers were awarded tin checks to reflect the value of their shopping bills and when they had collected large numbers of checks they would return them to my sister who would record the amounts in the customers' pass books. With nothing better to do, I was enlisted to count mountains of checks and bag them. Boring, but it filled in the time. I had spent so little time in my own home during the past six months that my mother and I had virtually ceased to communicate.

19th September, 1949

My dearest darling Ann,
I consider myself to be the luckiest boy in the world to know such a lovely, charming and generous girl as you my darling. You are so kind and gay and you give me all your attention and affection.
We have always talked about Hastings being our fondest memory but we must now surely include Blagdon. You were so sweet and brave in strange surroundings and I know that they loved you. But who doesn't love you? I forgot to ask you what it was like, sleeping with Auntie Floss. I was so proud to show you off to them.
I hope you feel the same way as I do about the past few days. I believe that we proved to ourselves that we can love each other without letting our physical emotions run away with us. It's thanks to

you for your control. I think that song is true ..Falling in love with love is falling for make-believe. What do you think?
  I love you so much,
  From your ever-loving husband to be,
  Arthur. xxx

21st Sept 1949

My darling Arthur.
Thank you for your lovely letter and the few days in Blagdon. We must thank them for having us but of course it was you who made the time so great. How can I thank you enough for the lovely times we have had.
  I do agree with you about the physical side of our love. I love you all the more for being so good to me. I shall always remember the walk along the river, when you were so loving and thoughtful for me.
  All my love from your future wife,
  Ann xxxx

My return from leave coincided with the start of 'Operation Bulldog', a two week national exercise testing home defences. This meant the re-introduction of night shifts, shorter off-duty periods and, worst of all, cancellation of all leave. An unexpected aspect was that only trained radar operators could man the radar equipment, leaving fighter plotters to be allocated to other duties. If I could have chosen a destination, it would surely be the tech site canteen where I could guarantee that my hunger pangs would be satisfied. And so it was ordained, much to the pleasure of Derek who immediately imagined a flow of surplus goods wending their way in the direction of our billet. Nobody seemed to notice that the canteen displayed greater numbers of sandwiches than usual, or that less margarine appeared on scones. But it all helped to equip the store cupboard in billet 13 A.

The success, or otherwise, of Bulldog was marked by the award of 72 hour passes for all concerned. But I was devastated to hear that I would be on guard duty for the whole of the next week, meaning that I would have to endure the longest period without seeing Ann, since joining the RAF, four weeks. Another reward offered by the Station Commander was authority for a camp dance to take place on the following Wednesday. I chose to go to Deal instead. There were no education facilities on camp and as my career in teaching was still uppermost in my mind, I went looking for the adult education centre for the area. With winter approaching, it would give me something to do during the long evenings. I signed up for three nights' attendance per week, studying Maths, Geography and French.

I was jolly glad that I missed the dance. Groups of girls were imported from Ramsgate, Deal, Ash and Sandwich and judging from the boasting that ensued, the local population was in for a boost. Two airmen faced charges for taking civilians into their billets, contrary to regulations, but I think that several other men were counting themselves lucky for not being caught.

Another community exercise was hastily arranged. There had been an increase in brushes with the law in Ramsgate, caused by heavy drinking by some of our airmen. Five of our officers lived in Ramsgate and challenged the police to a friendly football match, hoping that the event may sweeten the relations between us. In hindsight, we must have misunderstood the object of the exercise because we won 9-0 and I scored twice, even though I was the goalkeeper.

Eventually, my four-day pass was granted and I set off on my hitch-hike to London, completely unaware of the surprise awaiting me. I was lucky from the outset, getting a car lift from Ash Road all the way to London Bridge, giving me plenty of time to meet Ann at Stratford Place. After the usual banter with her friends, we decided to go to Leicester Square and have a 3s 3d meal in the Corner House. As we were walking in the Square, a voice suddenly called at my side.

"Airman!"

I froze, hurriedly wondering what I was doing wrong. 'Was it wrong to hold hands whilst in uniform?' An RAF officer stood in front of us. Instinctively, I saluted a half-hearted salute, slightly embarrassed in Ann's presence.

"Never mind saluting, airman. Will you do me a favour? I am unable to fulfil an engagement tonight and I'm looking for a couple who can use these tickets. You look smart, with your lady. Will you help?"

In the seconds that followed, I couldn't think straight. I had never spoken to an officer in public. Did I have to stand to attention? Should I offer him money? I had none, or very little. But he had disappeared. Ann and I stood gaping at each other.

"Better open the envelope, darling. Let's see where we're going."

It was the Aldwych theatre, dress circle seats, 7pm. We knew that we needed the Strand, but it was already 6.15. We dived into the Northern Line underground and aimed at Charing Cross. I found an evening paper in a rubbish bin on the platform and discovered that the show would be 'Tough At The Top' with Jimmy Edwards, one of my favourite wireless comedians. We ran the 200yards to the theatre, bought a bar of chocolate in the foyer and rushed up the stairs, just as the show was starting. It was an evening of constant laughter, made even more enjoyable by the surprise element. At the interval when the lights came up, we saw our neighbours for the first time and we laughed again. We were amongst the 'nobs' and we hadn't paid.

17th October, 1949

My Own darling Arthur.
How can I thank you enough for such a wonderful four days? Every minute was perfect, especially the surprise in London which even you couldn't have planned. Oh darling, how much I love you; life seems so empty when you're not here with me. You're so kind to me and I mean that from the bottom of my heart. I went to art classes last night on my shiny bike that you cleaned for me. Dad and Margaret thank you for cleaning theirs as well.
Darling, isn't life good to us? Especially love. I truly love you. How lovely it is to lie in your arms, quietly. Nothing worries me. I long for you to come home.
I shall have to finish writing now because I am in bed and can hear mum and dad talking about me still having the light on.
All my love from the future Mrs. Allwright,
Ann.

19th October, 1949

My darling Ann, the future Mrs. Allwright.
Thank you for the really loving letter. It was exceptionally nice to read because you must have been deeply in love with somebody when you wrote it. Only someone in love could write like that. In spite of what you say, I maintain that the good times we have are due to the kindness in your heart.
I am really in love with you darling and I'm sure we were made for each other.

No letter that I write to you
Says half the things I mean it to.
For how can words reveal a part
Of all the longing in my heart?
No pen and ink can translate this
The sweetness of a tender kiss.
Nor any word convey as much
As just a smile, a look, a touch.
How weak are words that can but say
I love and miss you more each day.

Isn't it a lovely piece of poetry, darling? And how true. But I'm afraid I didn't write it. I only wish I had. The person who wrote it must have been truly in love, like us. It expresses exactly what I've wanted to tell you for a long time and I'm glad I found this piece. You mean more to me than any of the words that I write.

Back at camp, two of us got the job of sweeping the leaves from the drive yesterday. Not my cup of tea, so we downed tools and went to a café in Sandwich. Then, to disguise how little we had done, we had a bonfire of the few leaves that we had swept. Sgt Platt was not fooled, however, and tomorrow we have got to join a firing party at RAF Hawkinge, near Folkestone, to practice rifle shooting on the beach. Don't go anywhere near Folkestone.

I'm glad you enjoy art classes. I think of you when I go to Deal with my studying. And, I also go on my bike, but mine's not clean.

While I was in Sandwich yesterday, I put £1 in the savings account. So I shall be able to buy you those chocs for Xmas, as promised! I love you my darling
From your ever-loving husband to be,
Arthur.

The rain certainly made its mark during October and November. The river burst its banks twice in one week, flooding the roads approaching the toll bridge. We began to think that the fields adjacent to Stonar would never rid themselves of the water. For two consecutive weeks we spent the evenings trying to dry our working clothes, only to get them soaked the following morning walking or cycling to the tech site. The officers tried to alleviate the problem by approving the use of our one lorry to ferry staff to and from the workplace. But just when we thought that the storms had cleared, another belt of rain arrived.

The bad weather was a reflection of other unfortunate incidents that have occurred. One such occasion concerned the sudden cancellation of passes for the weekend of the Armistice celebrations. A notice was posted that all ranks must attend the service of remembrance on camp at 10.30am on Armistice Sunday. Derek and I were furious and together with the other disappointed people intending to go on leave, we learned that we could leave camp but be back in time for the parade. I wrote to Ann telling her the news and said that Derek couldn't get to his home so she offered Derek the opportunity of travelling with me and staying at her place for the Saturday night. A lucky hitch-hike on the Friday and an on-time Saturday night train turned the weekend into an enjoyable arrangement. The annoying part was that during the parade, no roll call was taken, so we could have escaped the service without detection.

The food at camp had deteriorated over the past two months and the crunch came one evening when the quantity and choice of food was particularly bad. We were met at the dining entrance by a group of airmen who wanted us all to stage a sit-in and refuse to eat. We were apprehensive when the orderly officer arrived and instructed the sergeant to take the names of those complaining, i.e. all of us. The problem had been caused by the fact that rationing quotas had been cut and the cookhouse staff were finding it increasingly difficult to maintain standards. One man stood up and asked permission to see the CO, and to our surprise the orderly officer left the room and returned moments later with George, the Commanding Officer. He listened to the complaints and visited the cooking area, after which he asked us to return at 7.30pm when a supper of eggs, sausage and fried bread, normally a meal costing 11d in the NAAFI, would be available. He then undertook to investigate the problem, but insisted that no man under his command would go hungry. In return he asked us all to be patient and do our best in an imminent enquiry by visiting officers sent to analyse our working practices at the tech site.

Another last minute change of plans caused unease. Derek and I were amongst a list of fighter plotters and radar operators awaiting posting to other sites, some of which were abroad. The excitement of a short term abroad was mixed with the emotional turmoil of being separated from loved ones. Ann was aware of this and I had provisionally been told to take three weeks leave at the end of November pending a move to Malta. Then, suddenly, the posting was cancelled. My letter telling Ann of the good news was difficult to write, as half of me wanted to go. This attitude was reflected in Ann's reply when she made the same comment that an opportunity like this was unlikely to be repeated and it was a shame.

29th November, 1949

My own sweet darling Ann,
I hope that you have got over the bad news that I shall not be home for the three weeks leave for overseas posting. I agree with you that we shouldn't have been put through the heartache of expecting to be even further apart than we are now, i.e. being sent to Malta. I'm sure it's a lovely island, but only if we are going to see it together. In fact, we'll make it a date that one day we'll go there and see what I missed.
We had a bit of fun last night. Derek and I were a bit bored and he went into the next billet and 'borrowed' their wireless without asking. When they returned from Sandwich and discovered their loss, they heard it playing in our room. Unfortunately Derek had gone to the ablution block for a bath. They went there and stole all his clothes, leaving him to come back in the freezing cold naked. Worse still, they locked our doors that he couldn't get in. Derek was furious and went banging on their door with just a black sock covering some of his dignity. We all ended up laughing, but I hope he doesn't get pneumonia. Good job nobody had a camera handy.
Anyhow, darling, I must rush to the post, so goodnight, I love you so much and I'm glad that we have escaped the six months apart. With all my love, from your future husband,
Arthur.

One of our friends had got into trouble on camp and had resorted to stealing money. In those situations the civil police are not involved and instead the RAF conducts its own court marshals. Several of us chose to be present at his trial which was carried out in our NAAFI. It was a harrowing affair when we felt that it was the low daily rate of pay that had driven this chap to steal. But the prosecution won and he was sentenced to 112 days detention at the RAF Colditz prison at Colchester. It brought home to us that we must not get on the wrong side of authority. Colchester had a chilling history.
There was worse news to come. With Christmas approaching all eyes were on the notice boards for the holiday rotas. Naturally, the long distance travellers might well volunteer for the dates, giving them

the opportunity to accumulate longer leave periods later. But there would still be a shortfall. Sure enough, my name appeared at the top of the list with three duties on Christmas Eve and late on Christmas Day. Our disappointment was apparent in all our December letters but the New Year would make up for it!

14thDecember, 1949

My Darling Sweetheart.
I still can't really believe that I won't be giving you your present on Christmas morning. This national service is a real testing ground for our love, isn't it? I found out today that there is a plus side to it. Those taking leave over the New Year will get an extra two days, because of the duty rotas at the tech site. So I'm looking at this advantage to get me over the disappointment.
I've been reading some of your old letters and your affectionate words of love haven't changed since the first day I joined up. You really are a DARLING. Guess how many letters you have written?
91 letters, and with my mathematical brain, that means 364 sides of paper, approximately 5460 lines, 38,220 words using 6 or 7 pads of paper, and spending 18s 11d in stamps. When I consider that we are talking about eight months or 32 weeks, six of which were full leave periods, and with only four days in a week that I'm at camp, that means you wrote 91 letters in 92 days parted. I thought you would be interested!!
But seriously, every word tells me how much I am loved by you.
I have been out with the boys. Last Saturday five of us went to see Sid Milward and his Nitwits at the Palace theatre in Ramsgate. That was a good laugh. I needed it. I'm glad you enjoyed the outing to the London Lyceum with Margaret.
I'm going to read some more of your letters before going to bed.
With all my love, from your future husband, who is desperately in love with you,
Arthur.

I arranged to phone Ann on Christmas Eve. In retrospect it was not one of my better decisions. The chat was cheerful enough at the start, but after Ann had told me of everything that she and the family had done in preparation for the holiday, there was silence and I could detect that she was crying. It was ages before she could bring herself to carry on.

"Darling, I'm not as happy as I sound. I can't imagine waking up tomorrow knowing that you won't be round to kiss me. I hate the RAF for keeping you away. It's not fair." And she burst into tears again.

I felt helpless but was glad she couldn't see my wet cheeks.

"I'll make it up to you," I blurted out, not even thinking of how this could be. We'll have longer together next weekend." That's how the call ended, and neither of us had really enjoyed it.

25th December, 1949, Christmas Day.

My True Darling Ann.
My thoughts are with you today, even more than usual. It seems strange that a day of merrymaking comes along and we are not together to join in. But our turn will come. And this Christmas will be the only one in our lives that we shall be apart. I promise you that we shall celebrate EVERY Christmas together until the day that one of us dies.
I must hastily thank you for the lovely surprise this morning. I jumped out of bed, turned on Jim's wireless that he has lent me, and opened your card. You can imagine my surprise when I found those six lovely photos of my darling sweetheart. It's hard to choose which one I like the best. I think it must be one of the full face ones to see your smile. You are so beautiful.
After breakfast, where everyone ate very gingerly, for fear of spoiling their lunch appetite, I received the letter that you wrote yesterday. We are so close. Then I went to a small Methodist Chapel in Sandwich with another lad. There is a huge organ there and the organist is blind. Actually he is a jazz pianist in a local group. He is a remarkable person, knowing every tune in the hymn book, the number of verses and sings all the words. Consequently he gets a lot of tone and understanding in his playing.
Then it was for the big do at camp where, as tradition has it, the officers wait on the other ranks for Christmas dinner. CO George and Pilot Officer Bick did the honours and very well, too. Twenty one of us had the two of them running around getting the menu cards autographed by everyone. We all had four bottles of beer and fifteen

cigarettes, which in my case, will be used for buying favours. Three hours later it was tea time but nobody was interested. A few minutes ago I went to the dining room for a drink and someone had discovered that we had forgotten to cut the Christmas cake. So that will be part of tomorrow's action.

I love you so darling. Although I am having a merry but quiet time, I miss you so much and I want to be with you all the time. Goodnight my sweetheart. I hope you are like me and not over-eating!

With all my love, knowing that, in the New Year, we are assured that this enforced separation will end. I love you my darling,
 Arthur.

CHAPTER 6

Christmas 1949 was about to slip into history. It would expire in the same manner that it had started, quietly. Christmas day had been enjoyable enough with the other captives, but we didn't really figure in each other's long term ambitions. Some of them drank their way through the day and evening. It wasn't my choice. She was ninety miles away. I shared my day with her by writing one of my longest letters of love. The decorations that I hurriedly put up after Derek had gone home melded with the carols emanating from the crackling wireless that I had borrowed from Jimbo. As I gazed at the framed photo of Ann, the words of adoration flowed from my pen. I was with her in spirit.

My guard duty spell began at 8pm. In twelve hours time, the cause of our separation would be recorded as complete, and I could start planning my next trip due in a week's time to see my very lovely Ann. The duty officer Bick had just been to wish me a Happy Christmas, again, hoping that I would give him a peaceful night. But the guardroom was destined to be anything but peaceful. The phone rang at ten past midnight. It was the toll bridge custodian. No, he didn't ring to wish us all the compliments of the season. He was a little more irate. He was reluctant to ring the police and thought that we might prefer to handle the situation ourselves. Five men from the camp were causing a commotion on the river bank. Two of them had stripped off their clothes and were daring each other to swim across the river, not the most pleasant of challenges, considering the dirty appearance of the water at any time. My call to the duty sergeant left me with a problem. He was in the river party. In desperation, I called Bick, knowing that he was the only qualified lorry driver on camp. He was noted for his composure and politeness; these qualities persisted in this crisis. What crisis? Within minutes the lorry sped in the direction of Sandwich, a village proud to boast at least five illuminated pretend Christmas trees in windows around the harbour. Minutes later, it returned with its noisy Christians all singing their praises to God. All were oblivious of the RAF, but dry.

Boxing Day was seven hours old when I woke. It was just like any other winter day, cold with a brisk wind, but no indication that it was a time for merriment, well, not for me, anyhow. The BBC announcer wished me a happy Christmas and dared me to share it with my loved ones. But he added that we should remember those members of the armed forces not lucky enough to be with their families. Hell, that included me! But ….. why should it include me?

The brain worked overtime. I scrutinised the Southern Railway holiday timetables and let out an unstifled 'yes'. It could be done. Bick would have returned to his rented home in Ramsgate and nobody else would have cause to contact me. I could feel my heart racing at the challenge. Oh Ann, you give me such courage.

My relief guard, Jock, booked in early and I ran to the billet. A 'lick and a promise' wash had to suffice. I made a quick change into my best blue uniform to attract a sympathetic response from any kind driver; grabbed my back-pack, already bulging with the few presents that I had accumulated and I was away. A quiet word in the ear of Jock and the fifteen cigarettes allocated to us at the Christmas Day dinner, were sufficient to get a nod from Jock and a 'give my love to Ann, you lucky bastard.'

Plan 'A' was to stand on Ash Road near the railway station and if nothing had happened, then I would resort to the 10.15 to London.

But Christmas is a time of goodwill and Will came my way in the shape of a William Hardy lorry destined for Guildford.

"I can deviate a bit, I s'pose," mulled Ben the driver as we bypassed Canterbury. 'I've got all day, and it sounds as though you must be barmy in love, to do what you're doing."

Barmy or not, as I alighted from the cab at Bushey Road. I was almost there. Suddenly, my nerve left me. Suppose I embarrassed them by turning up unannounced. Would Ann really mind if I turned up with no ration card? Who else would be there and would there be enough food? I swallowed and plucked up courage. Walking down Greenway to number 59, I felt proud in my uniform with immaculate polished buttons shining in the winter sun. As I pressed the bell it was too late to turn back.

There was a scream as Margaret opened the door.

"Ann, quick. It's Arthur!"

One by one they hugged me. How could I ever have thought that I wouldn't be welcome. Ann kissed me, held me close, kissed me again, and laughed.

"What a surprise. Oh, I'm so excited." And as we kissed again, she whispered "I love you so much."

"We were about to have dinner, Arthur," joked her mum. "I suppose you can stay long enough to have some, before you dash back to camp?" And we all laughed. "It's cold turkey left over from yesterday. The bird was so big! Margaret won it with a bottle of posh whisky in a raffle at the bank."

Ann's dad lit a cigarette that he had just rolled. "You take the biscuit, Arthur. How do you get away with it?"

Margaret was as excited as Ann. "You always have a surprise up your sleeve. I wish my John wasn't so predictable. It's lovely to see you," and brushed Ann aside to give me another hug.

"Dinner's ready," called Ann's mum, "this afternoon we'll open presents, shall we?"

I wanted to give Ann her present now, I was so sure that she would like it. So I did and she let out a scream of delight as she unwrapped a pair of boots.

"Let me fetch your present," she said and rushed upstairs, returning with a beautifully wrapped gift with 'Love' on the paper. Inside was a large wallet for all my letter-writing implements. I was so pleased to have such a lovely present.

Dinner was a noisy affair with everyone talking at once. I was starving and readily accepted a second helping of turkey. But Ann hardly ate anything, content with asking questions about how I had managed to get away. When I answered she joked about me speaking with my mouth full.

"Give him a chance," said her dad, "he probably hasn't eaten for three hours." And laughter took over.

Within half an hour of clearing the table, both of Ann's parents had dropped off to sleep, leaving Ann and me alone in the front room. Our happiness was complete and we kissed and cuddled till our lips were sore.

"How long can you stay, darling?"

"All night, if they will let me sleep down here on the sofa. Then I can catch an early train in the morning. I must get back before twelve when the guard changes."

But time was rushing past. "I want to go round and see my family," I said. So we managed to squeeze in a flying visit, just five minutes walk away. I had presents for Mum and Dad, but nothing for my sisters, which equalled what they had for me, so we were all happy. Mum gave me some gloves and I just had time to tell them how I had managed to get home on this flying visit, before saying goodbye again and getting back to Greenway.

Everyone laughed when Ann asked if I could sleep on the sofa, but it was agreed. In the evening, Ann's relations and Margaret's John were due. I was very rude, however, and when Ann and I were allowed to sit in the front room on our own, I fell asleep in her arms. When I awoke, all the visitors had gone. Ann was so kind. Her left arm had 'gone to sleep' holding me, frightened to move, lest she woke me. She said that her auntie suggested that I had squeezed too much into one day and they had all agreed.

27th December, 1949

My very dearest sweetheart,
I don't know how to start this letter. Either I thank you for the most enjoyable twenty four hours of my life, or thank you for the lovely present, which I'm using at this moment. Even though it was very rude, it was like dreamland to fall asleep in your arms on the sofa last night. It was kind of you to stay with me all that time.
Please thank your family for making me so welcome. I wish I could have stayed for the rest of your holiday from work, but as you said, the day was stolen so we mustn't grumble.
I had a pleasant journey back, mixing sleep with entertaining two boys who kept coming from the next compartment to show me everything that Father Christmas had brought them. Oh, and the turkey sandwiches are still going down nicely.
It's nearly Friday and I shall be back for my Christmas leave. I love you so much and I'm so happy.
From your ever-loving husband to be,
 Arthur

Tuesday, 27th December, 1949

My darling Arthur,
I started writing this letter yesterday, but somebody came and interrupted me! I am hoping that the person will repeat the dose. I was so thrilled to see you and I thank you for coming all that way for such a short time to make me so happy.

I shall never forget the peaceful and loving sight, looking at you as you slept in my arms last night.
I can never thank you enough for my boots. I sat in the front seat of the 118 bus so that I could keep looking at my toes. My feet have never been so comfortable. Both mum and Margaret have tried them on, and want them!
I love you for ever. From your future wife,
Ann xxxx

The new year dawned with mixed expectations. There have to be unplanned setbacks. Otherwise, life would have no challenges. The first reversal came with the cancellation of all my evening classes due to lack of support. Not knowing how to keep on track for qualifications, I requested an interview with our education officer, Flt Lt Jackson based at Manston. He was impressed with my enthusiasm, but I detected that he was only too pleased to find someone with whom he could record actual educational assistance. He confessed that I was the only national service airman in his area trying to study. He suggested correspondence courses, but added that this would require a lot of self discipline. We discussed an offer from the Pitmans College in London, which seemed to meet my targets, but without saying anything I pointed to the cost per subject and shook my head.

"Don't worry about that," he said, "we'll set it up for you, but if you drop out without completing the course, I'll have to ask you to pay back the fees."

Tuesday evenings were suddenly removed from my studying calendar. Auxiliary Air Force personnel were being trained in fighter plotting at nearby Cliftonville and ten of us were 'volunteered' to help. We were taken by coach to a large hall that accommodated a replica of a plotting table similar to the one housed in our own operations room at Sandwich. The only difference was that at Cliftonville there was no radar, so the voices and instructions that we could hear on our headphones were related to imaginary flights. The auxiliary allocated to me was able to plug into the same 'jack' as mine and could then hear the instructions coming from the radar operator, and see the actions that I took. Unfortunately my companion was a giggly young miss who got on my nerves.

The volunteering bug struck again and I found myself with three others travelling to RAF Felixstowe, a seaplane base in Suffolk. Our task for a fortnight was to train some new recruits at nearby Trimley. The advantages of this posting meant superior food, an extra shilling per day and a lot of spare time. On the downside, of course, were two weekends without leave but with a compensating weeks leave at the end. Boredom during the middle weekend meant that we sat through a second viewing of the film in Felixstowe called 'The Spider and the Fly' with Eric Portman and a second film, William Bendix in 'Life of Riley.'

Ann had some good news for me on my return.

28th January, 1950

My own darling Arthur,
Guess what darling? I am now a model! Miss Newbury has asked me to accompany her when she goes out seeking orders for our dresses. Yesterday I modelled three dresses at two outlets and we got several orders. I don't know how much extra I shall get but she has promised me an increase.

As you won't be home this week, Pam from work will be staying with me on Sunday. We intend to have a 'sticking' day. We bind each other with sticky tape all over our bodies and it dries to our exact shapes. We can then use the dummy model when we make our own dresses. Good job you won't be around or we would have to lock you up. Now there's something for you to imagine next Sunday! On the wireless they are playing 'Saturday Night is the Loneliest Night of the Week.' It will be this week, darling.

I'm so sorry that you have lost your evening classes. I hope that nice officer will get you a correspondence course. You really are a darling to try and do well for me. Perhaps you will enjoy the Cliftonville training, although I don't believe you when you say that you couldn't stand the WRAF girl. You like every girl!

It's good that we can joke about these things, because we trust each other to be true, and I am really true to you. I want you as my husband, darling Arthur.
From your ever-loving wife –to-be,
Ann.

Derek thought that the dressmaker's dummy was a great idea.
"Wow! I'll get Shirley to make one of those and I'll bring it back here. I could cuddle it all night in bed and think of her."

"Calm down lover-boy. It's not what you think. Another girl would bind Shirley in a cloth from the neck down to just below the hips. Then, using a brown, thick, sticky tape, she would bind her tightly, picking out her shape. When the contraption is dry, they would cut the model down the back and Shirley would step out, all pink and sore. The cut would be joined with tape and she could then use the shape for dressmaking."

"You mean it would be hollow, and no legs?"

"Sorry to disillusion you, but yes, one big hole at the bottom; no use for what you had in mind."

"Bugger! I've gone off the idea," was all Derek could muster. But he envied me having a model for a girlfriend.

Valentine's day crept up on me and I had left it too late to get a card for Ann. So the quietness of the guardroom at 3am gave me the opportunity to express my love in a poem.

13th February, 1950

My own valentine, My darling Ann,
When you get this letter it will be Valentine's day, and the only cards you get will be from your other boyfriends like old 'long-neck' at the Art College and several of my football mates who, I know, adore you. My valentine words are in this poem, and although it sounds corny, it is sent with all my love.

The second month, the fourteenth day of every single year
The gentry of this country would put away their fear
And plucking up their courage, with ambition in their head,
Would go and seek their loved ones and suggest that they should wed.
The custom of St. Valentine is growing very old
So many modern people just think of it and scold.
But some girls wait intently because they think it's grand
To have a crowd of suitors all asking for their hand.
Bashful men who want to take advantage of this date
Will go and buy a heart-shaped card and send it to his mate.
Who seeing the 'guised writing, not knowing who it's from,
Will go and thank dear Freddie, but find it came from Tom.
Now I feel quite romantic but I haven't bought a card
So I shall have to put in verse, the words that aren't so hard.
And they are, that I love you, and I'll do the best I can.
If you will say you'll have me, my own sweet darling Ann.

You really are the only person I could love. You are never out of my thoughts and I talk about you to everyone I meet. That's the effect you have on me. So please be my valentine. With all my love for you always,
From your husband to be,
Arthur.

The CO had been informed of our visits to Cliftonville and the Station Routine Orders displayed on all notice boards, carried his congratulations, adding that those personnel should be excused from daily fatigues, excluding watch duties, on the following morning. Sgt Platt didn't take kindly to that, and his comment at the next parade was, 'I'll get you skivers some other way!'
He was true to his word. He caught me out one morning when I didn't think quickly enough and I found myself raising the flag, a task that was new to me. His sarcastic streak came to the fore and I had to report to the square at 10am to be given a lesson on the flag raising ceremony, much to the amusement of watching colleagues drinking their tea outside the NAAFI. In addition I was told to report to the transport compound where a load of coal had been delivered and required sacking into 1cwt bags. He had another surprise for me on the following day. Having found out that I was going on a five-day leave in a week's time, he selected me to be in charge of fire-lighting at the tech site in time for the morning shifts each day until my leave. This meant either having breakfast at 6am or waiting until mid-morning for sustenance. Neither suited me, but it taught me to get more organised with excuses.

On the third Cliftonville visit, we found that the officers had arranged a party for the Cliftonville auxiliaries. Nine of us attended and didn't cover ourselves in much glory. Each one collected a round of drinks from the bar, meaning that we downed eight pints. The outcome was that two of the gang were ordered not to go to Cliftonville again, after admitting that they had poured beer into an officer's cap. My main problem of the evening was to avoid the attention of the giggling WAAF girl who insisted in joining our group and sitting next to me. I didn't mind, but I was embarrassed each time she laughed at a joke her hand ended up on my knee, or higher.

Her ultimate scheming came when she confronted me in a corridor as I was returning from the lav. Before I could control my surprise, she pressed me against a wall and kissed me fervently, lips, tongue and teeth grinding away.

"Meet me in Ramsgate by the pier tomorrow night, 8pm, promise me. You are a real man."

I wanted to say 'no', but the wrong word came out. Unfortunately, she had chosen the moment just as our lorry was leaving, to give me the challenge. I had never been kissed like that and it caught me off-guard. To say 'no' would be lacking bravado, so the word remained unsaid. The beer ruled my vocal chords on the return journey and my enjoyment of the whole evening, according to the lads, was obvious. I crept into the billet intent on not waking Derek. I didn't want to be engaged in conversation about the party. Already, the pangs of guilt were beginning to gnaw at my aching head. Sleep rescued me temporarily from the solution cul-de-sacs in my brain.

I was bad company when I awoke. Derek suggested that the beer had not agreed with me and that I should get some food inside me, but even at breakfast, I was silent. Half of me wanted to forget the date for the evening and I was ashamed of the other half. But my saviour came from an unexpected source. Sgt. Platt was at his worst, at the flag-raising ceremony, dishing out work allocations with a venomous tongue. I was apparently slow coming to attention as the flag fluttered upwards and was immediately awarded a guard duty for the evening. My excuse for missing Ramsgate was a god-send.

Guard duty proved to be more eventful than the previous evening, bordering on insanity. It nearly saw the start of the great fire of Sandwich, 1950. The night was particularly cold and the fire in the stove chose to be obstinate. I was trying to concentrate on a general introduction paper to be submitted to Pitmans but the fingers were resisting movement. Occasionally my mind drifted in the direction of Ramsgate where Rose was probably shivering with cold, rather than expectancy. The bad half of me regretted the missed opportunity, but the real me was trying to benefit from the sparse heat of the stove.

I had used all the sticks and the coke required more draught to keep it alight. There appeared to be a blockage in the chimney, judging by the continuous smoking and fumes in the room. In a desperate attempt to get warm I shook the stove without success. An unorthodox remedy was called for. By climbing onto a stone wall outside the guardroom I was able to get to the roof and apply several sharp whacks with a broom handle against the metal chimney. I was unprepared for the result. A sudden whoosh sent showers of sparks and soot into the moonlit sky and there was a rumble in the room beneath me. If the outside display surprised me, then the sight below was shattering. Through the open door came clouds of smoke, accompanied by a stench of fumes. A pile of burning soot filled the area around the stove and several items were smouldering, including my study papers, the soft furnishings and tables.

I was close to panicking. I threw my two books and work papers onto the path outside and kicked a piece of smoking coal through the door. The room was getting progressively hot, due to the fact that my original objective of clearing the chimney had now taken effect and the increased draught was drawing the fire into life. At a time like this, I needed a friendly face and a person with a clever brain. The orderly sergeant who happened to be on patrol could boast of having neither of those qualities. He acted quickly enough to rid the room of the hot embers thus limiting the damage, which seemed to be his main plan. But he then turned aggressive, putting me on a charge of attempted arson which would be confirmed after he had sorted out the confusion. In the meantime, he ordered me to remain on duty while he aroused an unsuspecting airman to take over my position. On his return, with Derek, I was marched to the officers mess where the orderly officer would be found. To my surprise, the officer who appeared was not from Sandwich, but a stand-in from Manston, my education advisor. There could be only one result of this coincidence and it took Flt Lt Jackson just five minutes to hear my tale and dismiss the sergeant. Derek had almost completed the clearing-up of the mess in the guardroom when I re-appeared to finish my shift but we remained together for the rest of the night, apprehensive of the action that the sergeant was likely to take to get his own back on me.

"While you were at the officers' mess I made an entry in the guard report book for the last time that I was on duty, reporting the fact that the fire wouldn't burn and that the chimney required sweeping."

"What good will that do?" I asked.

"Well, as nothing was done, it was somebody else's fault that the guardroom was cold. It can only help."

"Thanks, mate, you're a pal. I owe you a pint.

As I lay on my bed in the cold billet, my mind turned to Rose. I may have escaped the turmoil for a while but we would still come face-to-face during the next Cliftonville visit. Surely I could think of a good tale. Why not tell her that I already have a girl friend? The problem had not been solved by the time that sleep overcame me.

My week's leave proved not to be the happiest period of our lives together. Two unexpected birthday parties enabled us to meet many of our friends. At the second party I couldn't help steering Ann away from one of the cricket team, Alec, who was holding her a bit too close.

"Keep away from Alec. I don't like him. I know what he's up to."

"It's not fair, you bossing me about. We weren't doing anything and he's funny. Don't spoil tonight."

"He was just the same on Tuesday at the other party, holding you like that. I didn't say anything then, but I was cross."

"If you're going to be like that, I'm going home." And Ann stormed out of the room to get her coat.

The abruptness of her action brought a deathly hush to the room and several friends asked us not to go. But the damage was done and even I couldn't paper over the cracks. My jealousy had embarrassed not only Ann and me, but also our friends.

Our walk home was punctuated with abuse.

"You don't seem to realise that my life while you are away, is like being in a convent. All I get in return is a spoilt night. Thank you very much. Why don't you go back to your camp, and don't bother writing."

By the time that we had arrived at her garden gate, we had calmed sufficiently to agree to go ahead with two planned visits to Wimbledon Common and Hampton Court both of which should have given us hours of ecstatic enjoyment. The Wimbledon Common visit passed off peacefully. But at Hampton Court, the problem of my jealousy resurfaced. Instead of accepting Ann's version about the innocence of the whole affair, I let jealousy rule my tongue and again said many unkind things. The argument became more and more heated until we suddenly realised that we only had three days of my leave left. We sat quietly in the grounds of Hampton Court, neither of us capable of bridging the gulf that I had created. The early Spring sun was threatening to leave the sky and trying to tell us something. Ann must have seen the message that we cannot go back in time. The past would be lost for ever; we cannot un-say anything. Repair and forgiveness is the only way forward. It was then that she blurted out about a secret she could hide no longer. She had bought tickets costing eight shillings and sixpence for The London Palladium to see a variety show on my last evening.

I felt terrible. How could I be so rotten and lacking in tact? Our eyes met for the first time in hours and tears welled up. Our arms went round each other and my ensuing words that I was determined to control my jealousy was genuine and we kissed on my promise.

We went to the theatre, happy that we had regained our love. Our fingers remained entwined throughout the show, parting only to applaud the fantastic acts. We laughed until we cried at the antics of a popular duo, the Bernard Brothers, whose miming of the Andrew Sisters was unbelievable. We ached with laughter, so much so, that on our way home we couldn't understand why other people in the train did not look as happy as we were.

Although my leave ended on a happy note, I returned to Sandwich feeling deservedly guilty and confided in Derek, giving him the gaudy details of my jealousy.

"I thought you two had sorted yourselves out," he replied. You always seem to take life as you find it. For God's sake man, if you keep up this Doubting Thomas role, you'll be a dead duck. You're not the best man in the world and she knows it. So don't give her an excuse to find out that Alec is better than you."

Why was Derek always right? This wasn't the first time that he had got me out of trouble, so I'd better follow his advice. I let the pen go to work.

1st March,1950

My Sweet darling Ann,
You were so kind on my leave in spite of the terrible way that I treated you. I meant my promise that I will respect you as you deserve. We should be so happy when we are together. I love you more and more each day. The one thing that keeps me going at camp is the thought of a sweet girl waiting at home for me. She is so generous and never puts herself first like most other people. When I come home for good, I shall always put you first, as you are now, in my mind.
It's a lovely day here today and four of us cycled down for a swim in Sandwich Bay. It's all private along the beach and we weren't supposed to be there. But the season hasn't started, so we weren't seen, we hope. It made me think of the holiday that we are planning for July, darling. Let's hope the sun is kind to us. Why can't we be

together on days such as this? I hope we get a good reply from Sandown and Ventnor.

It's lights out now, so it's also good night darling. Stay well and happy. I love you so much, from your ever-loving husband –to-be,
Arthur.

Ann's letter of the same date was startling and unexpectedly deflating.

1st March, 1950

Dearest Arthur.
I say, 'dearest' because you are. There is nobody in my life except my family, and there never will be.
But I cannot describe the hurt that you did to me last week and I don't deserve it. I accept that I was joking with the others at the party but that is all. You say that your jealousy will be controlled but it had better not show itself again. I would rather live lonely than keep wondering whether or not you are watching my every move.
I cannot write anything else tonight. I am too unhappy.
From the girl who wants to be your wife,
Ann.

I lay on my bed and agonised over the letter. I had over-stepped the mark and would probably regret my childish behaviour for the rest of my life. We had argued over my jealousy on a couple of occasions, but we had ended up laughing about it, because, deep down, I knew that Ann was true. But this was different. How could Ann have written such an ultimatum unless she meant it? How can I pretend that I wouldn't worry if she went out with somebody else, when all the time I would be absolutely torn to pieces inside my head?

I tossed and turned all night, seemingly getting no sleep. Derek knew that a letter had upset me but I refused to discuss it. In the morning I tore up my completed leave pass ready for signing, as I could not face Ann until I had sorted out what to do. The target was not in doubt, but how could I balance the undying love for Ann with my unjustified questioning of her love for me?

And what about Rose? Surely, this could be Fate punishing me for my behaviour.

CHAPTER 7

Ann didn't write for three days. I knew that she was under pressure at work and Winnie's wedding dress was taking all of her time at home. I wanted to believe that those were the reasons for not writing, but I sensed that she was still cross and determined to make me pay dearly for my behaviour.

I awoke on the Thursday in a new frame of mind. An early night had helped and common sense was at last penetrating my obstinate brain. The sooner I could get my pen to write the correct words, the better. I reported sick with dizziness. This ensured that I would be excused duties, giving me time to get a letter written and posted.

The objective of the apology was to reflect my innermost wishes, that of accepting full responsibility for the behaviour and subsequent abuses. I had reminded myself that Ann's undoubted sincerity in her love for me made little room for her to even want to stray. But, if she did, she would have judged that the other fellow must have better long-term qualities than me. In those circumstances, my recent performances would have contributed to that assessment, just as Derek had predicted.

I was not completely honest in my letter to Ann. I had intended to joke about Rose's intervention, but that episode had to be nipped in the bud and not allowed to develop. The event must never be allowed to surface in conversation.

After two re-writes, and convinced that I had achieved the correct humbleness, the letter of attrition was complete and I cycled into Sandwich to catch the lunchtime post. Such was my excitement on my way back to Stonar, that I returned to the post office and sent a telegram to Ann.

4th March, 1950
Ann. Letter in post. I Love You. Arthur

Ann's letter was on my bunk when I arrived back at camp. I was overjoyed at its contents. She wanted me home for the weekend, to make it all happiness between us. And she had written without seeing my apology. I reminded myself about how lucky I was, and the importance of overcoming my jealous streak. A box of chocolates was a must, to show my appreciation of Ann's generosity.

I was so overwhelmed by Ann's letter that I read a paragraph to Derek on his return from the tech site.

"Sounds like a reason for celebration," he said, rubbing his hands. "NAAFI or Sandwich?"

"It'll have to be NAAFI. I'm broke," I replied, "but not broke enough that I can't stand my social advisor a pint and a supper."

Two beers calmed my nerves and blinkered my conscience sufficiently to allow me to forget the agony that had kept me awake during the two previous nights. I slept soundly but the guilt was still present on three fronts when I awoke next morning. Not only was there another smashing letter from Ann, but also a letter from Pitmans enquiring about the non-submission of the final paperwork that would decide whether or not they would accept me as a student. Then, at parade, I had to explain why I had missed the Cliftonville visit on the previous evening. The latter omission was a punishable offence and Sgt. Platt had no hesitation in awarding me weekend guard duty, coupled with the stinging aside that I would be searched for matches before being allowed near the guardroom. That comment brought a howl of banter from the parade. The fun was lost on me because I was in deep trauma at the prospect of telling Ann that I wouldn't be home. As the parade was dismissed, John (Clown) Prince called out.

"Someone was asking about you last night. Someone named Rose. Any idea what she wanted, as if I couldn't guess. What have you been giving her Lefty? She's a bit of all right, ain't she? Lucky bastard. Hope you take your balloons from the Medical."

I left the parade ground feeling sick. Why did it have to be the Clown who found out about me. The story would be all over the camp within hours, and I hadn't even thought about Rose.

"What's this about Rose?" Derek prodded me in the ribs, his eyebrows raised. "No wonder you've been keen to go to Cliftonville."

"It's not like that at all," I replied. "You know I told you about that pain of a WRAF girl who kept giggling? Well, it's her. When we had that unexpected party at Cliftonville before Christmas, she caught me coming out of the bogs, just as the lorry was about to bring us back here. She threw herself at me and gave me the mummy and daddy of all kisses. Laugh if you want to, but when I broke loose she made me promise to meet her the following night in Ramsgate. If you remember, that was the evening that I volunteered for guard duty to avoid going to see her. It was the guardroom on heat, not me! And I've not seen her since."

"She's obviously keen to see you. Probably she wants to give you a bashing for leaving her to get cold in Ramsgate. You'd better keep your distance."

"Well I can't keep doing fatigues just to avoid her. Anyhow, I like going there. It gets me off parade the following morning, giving me four hours to do my study work. I'm behind in that area already. Got any ideas?"

We got on with the task of cleaning the billet, in silence. Suddenly, Derek threw the duster in the air.

"Got it! Offer Rose to Clown Prince." Silence returned while we thought about it.

"You clever bastard," I yelled, in relief. "That's it. He's the randiest bloke on site and he's just packed up the daughter of the King's Arms landlord. That's why he's started going to Cliftonville. If he falls for it, it'll keep his mouth shut about me. I'm really not interested in her, or anyone else for that matter."

I knew where to find Clown, in the NAAFI, having cheese rolls. Within minutes of tracking him down, I was back in the billet.

"You're a genius, Derek. But I think he had already set his sights on her, or perhaps even bonked her last night. He needed no encouragement from me, just confirmation that he didn't have a fight on his hands."

With the solution of that problem, there remained the greater issue of telling Ann that I wouldn't be home tomorrow. The only way of doing that was the telegram.

Ann had mocked me once or twice, jokingly, about a protruding tooth. It didn't worry me, the tooth, that is, but if the sight affected her, then I had to act to make sure that absolutely nothing upset her, however painful. Consequently, I made an urgent appointment with the Manston dentist to have an inspection. The ensuing sacrifice started half a day prior to the removal booking. No food was a nightmare. The operation was as bad as I had expected. The upper tooth was deep-rooted and when the second cocaine injection was proving ineffective, the kind dentist tried a third dose. I felt sure that he was pulling my head inside out. Eventually, the tooth gave in, but the sadistic actions had twisted the two adjoining teeth, necessitating re-alignment, giving yet more pain. Where was Ann to hold my hand?

It was her idea after all. To cap the whole episode, I had to stay in the Manston hospital for twenty four hours and was given a no-solid diet for two days.

On the brighter side, Derek and I saw an advert for dancing classes at the Sandwich village hall on Monday evenings. Neither of us could dance and we thought this would be a way to surprise our girl friends. I thought that I could fit it in with my studies. On a freezing evening we arrived at the hall, to be welcomed by the caretaker who told us that we were just in time for a talk about the United Nations! The dancing classes had started the previous Monday but as only one person turned up, the scheme was scrapped.

There was more good news on the money front. Occasionally, we were allowed to query our pay details, and following a tip-off, I managed to get a payment of £2.16s 8d for ration money that had not been paid for two of my official leave periods. Consequently, on the following Thursday, my pay packet swelled from the normal 9s per day to an enormous £5.19s 0d for the week.

The Rose episode died a natural death. I was apprehensive as I arrived for my first confrontation with her, but I needn't have worried. Neither she or the clown attended for two weeks, by which time they were clearly involved with each other. Rose even arranged to have her tuition from Clown instead of me and her only words as she brushed past me, were, 'you don't know what you are missing.' She was right, but that's the way I wanted it. One close shave of nearly losing Ann was enough.

The following weekend, I was at last able to see Ann and please her by saying that I had been accepted by the Pitmans College in London to take on their correspondence course in Maths, English Grammar and General Knowledge. The papers for each subject gave a proposed timetable leading to the first exam. I estimated that I would have to give up at least eight hours per week to meet that target. The Manston education officer was right when he warned me that I would need plenty of self-discipline. The list of books to cover the required reading was approved by Manston and Ann's dad said that he would give me an old copy of Whittaker's Almanac to help with the general knowledge subject.

Winnie came for the final fitting of her wedding dress whilst I was there and I was amazed at the beautiful creation that Ann had made. I asked her to hold it up against herself so that I could picture our wedding, but she refused.

The thought of being married was constantly in our minds and on the Saturday, we were given tickets for The Ideal Home Exhibition at Earls Court. Naturally, besides gorging ourselves on the give-away tasters, we collected mountains of brochures relating to our future home. After the excitement of the day, we got carried away and dallied too long on the way home, resulting in Ann being lectured for being late. We spent the Sunday in a difficult atmosphere, preferring to make progress with a small rug that we were making from a kit.

On my return to camp I felt guilty that Ann got all the blame and wanted to comfort her.

21st March, 1950.

My darling sweetheart.
I want to tell you about a lovely girl with whom I am deeply in love. You may know her. She is Ann Cobbett. She is very pretty, about 5ft 9ins, mousey hair, with a shiny ginger tint; slim with soft tender skin that gives a wonderful feeling to any boy that knows her. Her manners are always of the best, while her kindness and generosity to me is something unseen in other girls. She dresses smartly and brightly with modern fashions and is clever enough to have made most of her clothes herself.

Having glistening eyes and a perpetual welcoming smile on her soft enticing lips she is admired by all. That is why I am proud to say, 'Ann is my girl and future wife.'

There will be unsurpassable times ahead of us darling so I hope that we don't get old too quickly. I want us to be married and left alone to enjoy ourselves without worrying about the time. I am sorry that you had to be told off on Saturday, when it wasn't your fault. I should have considered you first, instead of encouraging you to walk the long way home.

I am so in love at this moment; I just want to hold you and comfort you.
From your ever-loving,
Arthur, your future husband.

Ann's reply was equally full of love and told me of an invitation to Winnie's wedding for both of us, but there was also bad news. Ann had written to several addresses to try and fix up a week's holidayin July. Now she had received some replies and she enclosed the letters from the Isle of Wight which drew blanks for our holiday plans and a disappointing note from Mrs. Givens in Hastings, saying that she would welcome us if we arrived with another couple. She was not keen to have an unmarried couple like us, alone. Neither of us wanted to share our holiday. Our time together was too precious. Unless we found some new addresses we would have to spend my July leave at home.

In her next letter, Ann reminded me that I had been in the RAF for exactly one year.

28th March, 1950
My very dear Arthur ... I cannot believe that it is only a year since you joined up. We have been parted for so long, it seems an eternity. My life is empty without you at my side. This poem was in last night's London Evening Standard.
'My Love For You

Spring is in the air.
But what's the use
If you're not there?
Birds sing, sun shines
But without you
My heart still pines.
Send fog, send showers
If you are here
There are no dreary hours.

I can only cling on to the fact that we are two thirds of the way through your RAF service. Promise me that we shall never ever be parted again. Love and miss you so much.
From your ever-loving wife–to-be,
 Ann.

Yes, Ann was right. The eventful year really put pressure on our love for each other. I had originally feared that I would lose her to one of the other admirers at home, and my recent outburst had taught me a lesson. Hopefully, the pangs of doubt would subside. Her art school gave her an interest while dressmaking kept her busy at home, to compensate in a small way for not having a more exciting social life.

I accepted the inevitability of serving in the RAF together with the associated discipline. I had been unexpectedly lucky with the amount of home leave. This was due to the fortunate posting to non-operational Sandwich. This was all about to change, however, and we would have to face the reality of restricted leave. With the exception of being parted from Ann, the short-term aspect of national service allowed me to enjoy the comradeship associated with it. The food at Sandwich was pretty abysmal but as long as I was prepared to supplement the main ingredients with thick bread and marg, I would not go hungry. So there was now only six months left to try 'beating the system'.

I noticed that there had been a sharp increase of airmen at the camp. This was due to the approaching date for the opening of our new operation centre. Although this meant that there were more people to carry out daily duties, there were also more jobs to do. The large ops floor was covered with brown lino; just suitable for the back-breaking work of polishing it. A favourite description of the orderly ops sergeant was, 'I want to able to see my face in it.' Our retort was 'I shouldn't bother, sarge, it's not that pretty.'

Two birthdays had to be celebrated at camp and the most popular way was at the dart board in a pub. The Kings Arms was the most fancied of the thirty two pubs in Sandwich. None of us had much money but we were pretty good with the arrows. Consequently, there was a growing tendency to challenge the locals on the basis that the losers would pay for the drinks. I had the advantage of having played regularly with Ann's dad at weekends, and was full of confidence. At the second birthday the landlord provided a buffet and I had to play the deciding rubber of two games against the captain of the pub's darts team, to decide whether the airmen or locals paid for the drinks and food.

The pub was noisy enough when I won the first game of 501 with 13 darts, but when I repeated the dose with 15 darts in the second game, going out from 102, the place erupted. We drank heavily that evening and I was carried back to Stonar House shoulder high. I was fortunate to escape being thrown over the toll bridge into the river.

Leave was cancelled for two consecutive weekends to facilitate preparations for the AOC's inspection, an annual event, and the forthcoming 'Stardust' exercise. When we were not on watch, the floors of the operations room had to be washed with paraffin and polished. Those of us chosen for the guard of honour for the inspection had the additional task of rifle drill and marching. Much of the marching was through the Sandwich streets, with plenty of banter from the local youths.

Our billet had its Spring clean during which time we discovered the cause of a smell in the room. Rats had gnawed a hole in the floor behind the wardrobe and food remnants had rotted.

No sooner had we finished the clean-up, than forty eight radar operators arrived at Stonar to assist in Stardust. One was allocated to each room, irrespective of space availability. With three in our small room, two of us had to climb over the other beds. Fortunately, our new room-mate, Jim, was friendly, and accepted our house rules about walking on our polished floors with pads under his feet and keeping the place tidy.

The Easter weekend interrupted the Stardust rehearsals but leave was restricted to two days. Hitch-hiking was unusually difficult with so many airman all crowding the Ash Road. In an effort to overcome the problem two of us went to Ramsgate hoping for better luck along the Thanet road. This was a bad move, resulting in wasting the day and not seeing Ann. She had arranged for me to play football on the Saturday, leaving us just a few hours together before rushing back to camp. Neither of us was pleased with this.

12th April, 1950

My own sweet Ann,

I'm so sorry about the weekend. I should have cried off from the football even though it would have let the team down. You are more important than them. I won't play any more this season.

I got back here just in time to go on watch Our times this week are 1pm – 5pm and 9pm – 1.30am. Next week will be even worse, 9am – 1pm, 2pm – 5.15pm and 9pm – 1.30am.

It looks as though we shall only have time for two meals per day, breakfast and tea.

Derek and I are going to the pictures in Sandwich tonight. Gregory Peck is in 'Twelve o'clock High'. Don't worry. We never sit in the pictures holding hands. I wish that it was you and me going out tonight. All my love.

Arthur.

14ᵗʰ April, 1950

My own darling Ann
It's not very often that I write to you at this time of the morning. It is only 8am and already I've been on a five mile run, in the rain, had a bath, (the second in three days, dirty thing), and went to breakfast. But although I was first, there were only kippers which I hate, so I had to put up with bread and marmalade. You are probably at Waterloo at this minute.
I'm glad you and your mum and dad enjoyed the Palladium. Lucky you, seeing the Bernard brothers again. Didn't they make us laugh when we saw them?.
I've had the first results of my maths test. 68%. Not bad because I know that I shall do better next time with more revision.
Hope you like the chocs darling. I love you so much. I only wish I could watch you eating them.
My love and kisses are for you only, my darling.
From your ever-loving husband to be,
Arthur xxxxx

Things started hotting up in preparation for the AOC's inspection. The CO called for a special parade on a Saturday, just so that he could check on our guard of honour routine. Surprisingly enough, I enjoyed the marching and counter-marching. It must have been a relic of the West Kirby days when corporal Preston made us inch-perfect with every drill.

Following the parade, the CO made a spot check on the billets. He was amazed that we had three in our billet. He said that this shouldn't have happened, and instructed Sgt. Platt to sort it out. We had taken to Jim and his humour, so we told Platt not to move him. Jim thanked us by taking us down to the King's Arms in the evening where he treated all the tap-room customers to his rendering of a song "Welcome to the Wild West Show", in which Jim said a verse and we all joined in, singing the chorus.

His first verse got a roar of approval. 'The animal in the cage in front of you, is the Leopard . This animal has on his back, 365 spots, one spot for each day of the year.'
'Hey mister, what happens on leap year?'

' George, lift up the h'animal's tail and show the lady the twenty-ninth of February.'

After we had sung the chorus, Jim continued. 'The animal in the next cage is the Laughing Hyena. This h'animal eats once a day, craps once a week, and fornicates once a year. What the hell he's got to laugh about, God only knows.' The landlord loved that one.

Jim's third verse had the place in an uproar. 'The bird in the next cage is the Oo-me-gooly bird. This bird has no legs. It circles at five hundred feet looking for prey. When eventually he comes into land, he lets out a loud cry, from which he gets his name, …..Oo-me-gooly, oo-me-gooly, Oo-me-gooly.'

From that moment, we bought no drinks. By the time Jim had recounted fifteen verses, the locals from the lounge had heard the laughter and joined us in the tap room and insisted on keeping our glasses full. The landlord even arranged for us to be driven back to camp an hour after closing time.

Derek and I volunteered for a special Auxiliary watch on the Sunday. As I explained to Ann in a letter, this apparent madness was born of the premise that we might get excused work on the following weekend. But we were nearly caught out. In our drunken state after the revelry, we forgot to alter the clocks. Consequently, when we got the 8am call, we thought it was only 7am and went back to sleep. Eventually, we arrived at the tech site on time, but only by forgoing breakfast.

Jim came up trumps again. I was bemoaning the fact that Ann and I were having no luck in finding a holiday venue in July, because we were not married. Jim laughed, telling us to buy a ring and go and stay with his mum in Brighton. He offered to check some dates.

The weekend pass was approved and I had the prospect of a superb couple of days looming on the horizon. It was the wedding of Ann's friend Winnie, for whom Ann had made the dress. As we sat in the church in Brixton, hand in hand, Ann whispered that it was a pity that we would have to wait three years before it would be the two of us in this situation. We were bound to wait that long to allow Ann's dad to recover from financing her sister Margaret's wedding, due in a year's time.

The wedding dress was a hit with all the guests and I felt proud of the compliments being given to Ann. The success of the day brought Ann and me much closer again after my recent bad behaviour. Ann suggested that we should go to Hampton Court on the Sunday. It turned out to be a good idea. The spring sun was kind to us and we enjoyed reviving our temporarily lost love. I sensed that the worry over the dress had tired Ann considerably without her realising it. But now, that had passed and she was contemplating her next task of making a summer coat for herself.

The sun didn't last for long. On my hitch-hiking journey back to camp on the following day, I was caught in a snow blizzard, resulting in being charged for absent without leave for two hours. The CO was not pleased to see me on a charge, and ruled that, in view of my participation in the guard of honour, the charge was dismissed. My day was made even more eventful when I read a Pitman's report that I had achieved a 70% mark for English.

Thursday's letter from Ann brought some exciting news.

21st April, 1950

My very own Arthur.
I have some wonderful news .I have heard from that lady in Brighton that we can stay with her for a week in July. The terms for bed breakfast and evening meal will be £4. 4shillings. I am so excited and I hope you are too. Just think. We shall be together for a whole week on our own. I am so happy.
You made the weekend so enjoyable. You looked after me at Winnie's and everyone liked you. You looked so smart. Wasn't Hampton Court good. We have never been so happy. I am so lucky to have you for my future husband. I wanted it to be us walking down the aisle last Saturday, didn't you?
I have got the snaps of the wedding back from Boots. They are really good, especially the one of me by the church. Dad thinks you will make a good photographer.
I am the happiest girl in the world.
From you ever-loving wife –to-be,
Ann.

Ann had made me the happiest man in the world again but she could still twist me round her little finger. She had taught me a severe lesson and our future was now in my hands. But it would be my tongue that would require control.

CHAPTER 8

<u>To The Most Beautiful Girl In The World.</u>

My darling Ann I love you so, more than you could ever know.
While we're apart I'll always miss the sweetness of your tender kiss.
And when I sit and dream awhile, I think about your loving smile;
The beauty of your beaming eyes showing love that never dies.
So darling Ann, while I'm away I'll think of you both night and day.
But I'll return, my lover, true and give the best of all to you.

Derek was aware of my happiness and persisted in trying to find out what happened during my last weekend at home. "You are either well-blessed where it matters or you've got the gift of the Blarney. You don't deserve Ann."

I had to agree with him and confided that I had feared the worse throughout the weekend. I showed him the poem that I had just posted to her.

"Cor blimey, did you write that stuff? I can't. Can I have it to send to Shirley? That would guarantee me a bunk-up. Go on. There's a pint in it for you."

That was the easiest pint I had ever earned and we laughed as we remembered to delete Ann's name.

Ann's reply came within two days and captured the same poetic atmosphere.

3rd May, 1950
My dear darling.
Thank you for your wonderful poem that I believe really came from the bottom of your heart. You make me the happiest girl in the world. I shall now cheer you up. David has told me that there's a game of cricket on both Saturday and Sunday next weekend. You had better get your pass sorted out! There is also a social and dance on Saturday evening so you're all booked up for both days.

But you're booked up for ever in my heart, Arthur, just a permanent innings, darling and we'll always dance our way through troubles and joys together. Just you and me. I can't wait to have the last waltz on Saturday, so that we can be alone together.
From your ever-loving wife-to-be,
Ann.

Cricket was beginning to take over all my spare time and I kept telling myself that I would have to say 'No' more often. But at the moment, as long as I kept working at my studies, I could take advantage of the regular games in Ramsgate on Wednesdays and get the occasional game at home. I found myself getting quite friendly with Pilot Officer Groves, our Wednesday captain. He was a national service officer who loved cricket and it was his pressure on the CO that got the go-ahead for the station team to be formed. Some airmen with an in-built aggression towards officers, were unable to allow themselves to socialise, even on the cricket field. It was quite ridiculous, really, when they avoided throwing the ball to him to get the ball back to the bowler. On one occasion, 'Fingers' Carter, who was quite a good batsman himself, called for a stupid run and got Groves run-out. We were all convinced that he did it on purpose.

I found Groves to be very approachable and consequently, after a couple of games in which I had enjoyed a rare bit of success, he asked me to carry out the admin side of the team, contacting other RAF and local teams for fixtures. The icing on the cake was the additional responsibility of being responsible for the Sports Store that housed, not only cricket gear, but also hockey and football equipment and bicycles. This job took precedence over any 'fatigues' that Sergeant Platt allocated daily at the flag-raising parade. I became the envy of many, and a scourge of poor old Platt. I needed an assistant and although Derek didn't play any sport, he took on the mantle. The cricket bats were oiled continuously, pads were whiter than white and the two footballs were inflated and laced, ready for the call.

The store became my office and having the door key enabled me to do my Pitmans work and letter writing without being interrupted. There was an immediate improvement in the papers posted to Pitmans, with both English and Maths results giving me the pleasure of having marks consistently in the 80% region. Derek's contribution to our new home extension was to provide a small stove and frying pan. One of the store cupboards had a good cleaning and became the home for our basic cooking ingredients. We agreed that secrecy would have to be paramount. Nobody could be trusted and Sergeant Platt's informants would enjoy rocking the boat if they were not on board with us.

We had cause to celebrate on the first evening when Jim told us that he was leaving. We scrounged what we could from the cookhouse, and having locked ourselves in the store, enjoyed a respectable supper of sausages and fried bread, followed by breakfast cereal, trifle and evaporated milk. This was washed down with cups of beer. Then Jim suddenly remembered a cake that he had brought from home and this was duly despatched. Derek went to bed with stomach ache which he richly deserved after scoffing five sausages.

It was fortunate that we went to breakfast in the morning, because a notice had been posted in the cookhouse cancelling the morning site operation and replacing it with a guard of honour practice. Heavy rain didn't help and after two hours of marching and counter-marching, with intervals of rifle drill, we staggered, wet and bedraggled, to our billets, just in time to be told that we would be on duty afternoon and evening.

With the guilt of the pending weekend of cricket hanging over me, I cycled into Ramsgate to buy a present for Ann's nineteenth birthday. Shopping was not one of my pet loves so I was lucky to find a small gold-coloured locket for two pounds fourteen shillings in the first shop I tried. Derek thought that I had really guaranteed a good bedding, but I assured him that my only prizes would be on the cricket field and not behind the pavilion.

I met Ann and her workmates as they were leaving their sweat-shop opposite Lilley & Skinner in Oxford Street. I was always proud to be seen in my uniform and Ann often remarked about the flattering comments of her friends. But the thought of the locket in my pocket gave me an added excitement and this must have shown, judging from the cross-examination by Winnie and Elsie. They let us leave, only after Ann had promised to tell them everything on Monday.

My plan was to go to the Lyons Corner House, Leicester Square, where we could indulge in their salad bowl for 2s 9d. The attraction of London's new way of satisfying the 'inner man,' was that I could eat as much as I wanted for the set price. Hopefully, Ann would then agree to a walk in St. James Park, where I could give her the present. We were so happy and laughing too much for me to keep the secret, and I blurted out that I had something to give her. As she opened the box her face lit up and wanted me to fix it round her neck. But I was too shy in front of all the people so we agreed to do it properly at the spot in the park where I had proposed to her. We were like two tiny children peeping at their presents under the Christmas tree. Ann kept opening the box for a quick look while we were still eating and we kept laughing at our antics.

Our kissing in the park became more intense and only the constant reminder of the time and the necessity to catch our train, prevented us from going beyond the boundaries we had set ourselves. On our way home we talked about our forthcoming holiday and the need to control our feelings when we would have no time barriers. With Ann fingering her locket constantly, we promised each other to rely on the trust that her parents had in us, when they had agreed to the holiday arrangements.

The cricketing side of the weekend was a success. Both matches were for our Crusaders Boys Club and I scored over forty on both days. Most of the league matches were played on council pitches in Morden Park, Surrey, and, being dangerously uneven and worn, they favoured the bowlers. It was not unusual for players to be hospitalised, and one of the opposition had stitches in a cut eye. I must have been lucky, but my natural tendency to slog paid dividends and we won both games.

The Saturday dance in the local park pavilion, gave us the opportunity for more cuddling. Our prowess was limited to the waltz, quickstep and smooch, but everyone joined in the Veleta and Gay Gordons, The music was on 78rpm records played on an old wind-up gramophone and we took it in turns to select the tunes. Victor Sylvester and his dance orchestra was always a favourite but one of our club members worked at a nearby Decca Records factory, and had purloined a pile of faulty records for the club. Consequently, the gramophone needle often got stuck, always at the same place and this caused endless amusement. The last waltz, as ever, was the signal for all the shy youths who had not danced all night, to make a bee-line for the few remaining girls without partners, hoping to secure their snogging ticket for the walk home. For Ann and me, however, the last waltz was our chance to show our friends how much we loved each other.

On returning to camp, I learnt that one of our mates, Bernard had asked to replace Jim in our billet. Derek had put him wise as to the cost of such a move, but Bernard had done his homework and produced the necessary arm-twisting in the shape of three tins of beans, six eggs, a tin of apples, half pound of sugar, a jar of dripping, half pound of butter, half pound of marg, six rashers of bacon and a tin of evaporated milk.

We were facing a week of extended guard of honour rehearsals made worse by the introduction of a new rifle drill programme. The sequence was simple, but involved an exaggerated slow movement of the rifle at arms length, resulting in two airmen being ousted from the team with shoulder strain. For the remainder of us, it meant additional rehearsals while two new newcomers took over their roles.

Ann's Thursday letter was full of news.

22nd May, 1950.

My own darling Arthur.
What a lovely weekend you gave me. Even though it was cricket most of the time, I am the happiest girl in the world with that smashing locket you gave me for my birthday. When I showed it to the girls at work they all said that they knew you were up to something, by the way you behaved when you met me from work Friday.
There has been a heck of a row at home tonight. Margaret and John want to get married immediately, because John can get officers' quarters accommodation in the RAF. Mum and Dad are cross. They say that if anything goes wrong it will be up to them, (mum and dad), to sort it out. I put my foot in it by telling them that Winnie estimates that it costs them £4 per week to feed two. So how could Margaret find that sort of money? I left them to it. I didn't want to spoil the memory of our lovely weekend.
Mum has had an invitation for her Townswomen Guild to go on a tour of The Queen Elizabeth liner at Southampton next week. Lucky thing.
We've had a letter from the lady at Brighton. If you are prepared to sleep in a hut joined onto the house, she will reduce the price to three and a half guineas. I expect there will be a bed in there! What do you think? We won't be able to have our goodnight kiss will we? It's so exciting looking forward to our holiday.
Another big surprise, darling. Mr. Dimond next door said that you can phone me on Thursdays in the evening if you wish. All I have to do is to knock just before we expect you to phone. Aren't we lucky? Just

in case you can phone this week, I shall go in there at 8pm and wait ten minutes. Don't worry if you can't let me know if this is OK. I long to hear your voice darling.

With all my love .. from your ever-loving wife –to-be,
Ann.

In my excitement to make sure that I had sole use of the phone box at 8pm, I had forgotten to check the amount of change in my pocket. After the telephone operator had got Mr. Dimond's number, I inserted tuppence only, just to make sure that Ann was there. The operator then asked for more and I added one shilling and sixpence and said that was all the change I had. I was convinced that there was no 'click' on the line, which made me think that the operator was still listening to our conversation. This had happened before, and by making our talk more juicy, I hoped that he would give us extra time. The plan worked and we spoke for thirty-five minutes for one shilling and eight pence.

After the call, it was time to clean the buttons on my best blue uniform for the Whitsun break. The Scots had agreed to carry out the guard duties for the weekend so the rest of us chose our different ways to get out of Sandwich by Friday lunchtime, with passes to be away until Tuesday noon.

It was destined to be a strange weekend. Ann had to spend Saturday at her Italian friend's house to make some alterations to a wedding dress for the following Saturday, a wedding to which Ann, but not I, had been invited. So, although I had a cricket match for the Saturday afternoon, I had the unusual experience of being at my own house for the rest of the day. My sisters played on the idea that they didn't know who I was, and my mother thought that I ought to stay there for Sunday, when they were expecting two aunts and uncles and three cousins. Mum was pleased to get my ration card for the weekend and this softened the blow that I would be at Ann's for the rest of the holiday.

What I didn't tell my family was that Ann's mum and dad had gone to Hastings for a week and left Margaret with John and Ann to look after the house. John was not happy to see me early on Sunday as he obviously had set plans for the day. Ann kept the peace by offering to go out walking, leaving them alone, but insisted that we would be indoors most of Whit Monday. It was a hot day and we took a picnic to Hampton Court, finding a secluded spot in Bushey Park. We talked about Margaret and John, wondering how long it would be, before they married. We used sandwiches as a saving excuse to prevent our physical desires from taking over our priorities, but by the time we decided to make for the trolley bus, our lips were sore from kissing and Ann discovered that she had bites all over her legs and back. This was an unhappy ending to our day because Ann had suffered badly from bites on several occasions and we knew that she would end up at the doctor's surgery to get huge blisters pricked and treated.

Monday was not a happy day. The blisters had appeared during the night and the irritation was unbearable. John mocked us incessantly, wondering what we had been doing. We realised that he was only covering up his own activities, but it made Ann cross and the weekend ended like a battleground. Both John and I were in our uniforms on the Tuesday morning, ready to leave for our respective camps. Having slept on the front room sofa while he had been given a comfortable bed upstairs, I couldn't help making a stab at him at breakfast.

"Thanks for spoiling our weekend John,"

"Sir," he said.

"Not likely," I replied, "You aren't worthy of wearing that uniform."

Margaret didn't hear our exchange but Ann stepped in just in time as John threatened to charge me. I couldn't help laughing at him, but fortunately he shut up and left the room, slamming the door. Both Ann and I agreed that we would leave the matter there and not make an issue of it.

"He's typical of the national service officers that I've come across," I said, "and he's got the additional drawback of being an only child and got spoilt as a kid. Actually thinks he's superior. What?" I mocked.

A letter from Pitmans greeted my return to camp, enclosing exam papers for Maths and English that had to be submitted by 10th June. The possibility of meeting that target was enhanced by the King, although he wouldn't have known about it. His birthday would be celebrated on 8th June and the armed services were always given one day's leave. My diary was pretty full, although guard duty during the intervening weekend would prevent me seeing Ann and contribute some hours for study. Two Wednesday cricket matches, a Cliftonville visit and an unknown number of guard of honour rehearsals, would have to take priority.

I was determined to get good marks to show Ann that I could achieve qualifications for a good job. In the eyes of the RAF, John may be better officer material because of his background, but I would prove to Ann that I could make her happy and well-off.

CHAPTER 9

Dark clouds were gathering in my mind. Ann had announced, quite casually, that she and three of her workmates were going to Butlins Holiday Camp at Skegness for a week at the end of July. That would mean that one week after our return from Brighton, she would be away. It took words of wisdom from Derek to remind me of my undertaking just a few months previously, that I must curb my exasperating jealousy and not jeopardise my future with Ann by ignoring my trust in her.

"Look at it this way, Arthur, the worst thing that will happen is that Ann will have a good time, even if it's with other company. You have to assume that she will come home having had a bit of fun, but ready to get back to normal. If you rock the boat again, you'll be saying 'good-bye'."

Of course, Derek was right. Deep down, I knew that. I would never forget the close shave after the party when Ann gave me fair warning of the possible consequences if I let my jealousy rule my brain. Yes, I had to go out of my way to demonstrate my love for her and my wish that she must have a good time in Skegness, to thank her for being so true during all the boring months that I had been away. No innuendoes, no teasing and don't dwell on the subject, especially during our own holiday. Don't mention it in my letters.

10th June, 1950

My darling Ann.
What a wonderful weekend. You were so special all of the time, even when I was playing cricket on Saturday.
After leaving you, I caught the last train to Waterloo and walked to London Bridge. On the way, I came across two women fighting in Sumner Street. Two men couldn't keep them apart there was blood everywhere. Two policemen turned the corner and instead of sorting them out, they chose to ignore the women and hurried back in the opposite direction. I didn't blame them! A taxi turned up and one woman got in, but the men couldn't hold the second woman, who

jumped in and continued the fight. Goodness knows what happened next.

There's bad news at camp. Weekend passes have stopped and we can now have Tuesday to Thursday, Friday to Sunday morning or Saturday midday to Monday evening. We'll have to sort out which will be best for us. It's all caused by full time operations now and our shifts will be in two- five hour blocks with a meal break in between. We'll still get time off for sport, but Sergeant Platt will still have his fatigue parades in the morning for those not doing night work. It's all very complicated.

I've just finished sewing my cricket whites. The legs were too long, so I've given them turn-ups. Well, I had to do something, because we have several matches coming up and the captain had made a few comments. No cutting off the spare length ... proper turn-ups. You'll be proud of me lady seamstress! Also, I've bought some white socks in Sandwich, for three shilling and eleven pence.

I'm on duty in half an hour so I must get this letter ready for posting. All my love from your future husband, Arthur. Xxx"

It was going to be a very busy week. 'The Air Officer Commanding', AOC Inspection was scheduled for Friday and our guard of honour preparations would take up the whole of Thursday. But before that, there was the small matter of an inter-station knock-out cricket match versus Swingate, to be staged at Ramsgate on Wednesday afternoon. Pilot Officer Groves, the captain annoyed the regular team members by selecting two other officers to play and nobody knew how good, or bad they were. There were rumours of boycotting the game by several upset airmen, so a team meeting was called to sort it out. The problem was overcome by a promise that all regular members who were selected or went to the ground to support the team would be excused night duty on Wednesday.

The bribery worked. The lorry carrying the team to Ramsgate was full and included the three officers who joked with the men throughout the journey. This had a good effect on the morale and it was a happy team that took to the field. Despite two dropped catches by one of the officers, we dismissed Swingate for eighty five runs. We never found out whether or not the two officers could bat because I opened the batting with Pilot Officer Groves and we passed their total without being parted. We both scored forty not out.

The early finish to the match enabled me to lock myself away in the sports store and complete the General Knowledge paper for Pitmans. This was the last of the work to be submitted, and if my overall marks in the three subjects reached the 75% standard, then I would receive the certificate that would satisfy the entry to Goldsmiths Teachers Training College if I decided to proceed with their courses.

Thursday was a nightmare. The aircraft flight times for the day had been changed twice already and at breakfast a new schedule appeared. As the cricketers had missed the Wednesday night watches, we were awarded 9am-2pm and 3pm-8pm with a walk back to Stonar House for lunch during the break. Those of us involved with the guard of honour troupe, had the additional chore of cleaning our best blue, buttons, boots and rifle, ready for a 'run-through' at 6am on Friday. Strangely enough, the spit and polish of buttons and shoes was not a problem. The square-bashing training at West Kirby had instilled a pride in our appearance for formal parades. 'Bastard Preston' had always maintained that a shoddy airman would always make mistakes in a drill, and I had to admit he was right.

As the CO came down the steps from his office to inspect us at 6am, I was conscious of all the men around me, stretching their backs upwards, becoming inches taller, just because they knew that they looked smart.

"Parade ….. Shon!" and we came to attention as one man, as the CO walked along our lines. "Parade, you have done yourselves proud in your appearances. Please let it influence your drill for the AOC later. Sergeant, dismiss the guard, feed them well and get them out here at 1030hours."

And our appearance was reflected in our performance. The marching, counter-marching and rifle drill was executed silently, and without orders. We knew we were good and we accepted the plaudits of the AOC, with no signs of emotion. We were professional.

But we were human and there had been a method in our madness of putting ourselves through the pain for so many weeks. Three extra days leave to be taken at any time during the next month. I had already done my calculations. I could extend my leave for our Brighton holiday.

There were two letters from Ann on my bunk. I remembered having seen them the previous evening, but the chores had taken precedence and then I forgot them. In both letters she was asking me not to get leave at the weekend and if I could telephone in the evening she would explain. This was a coincidence, because Pilot Officer Groves had cornered me as we jumped from the lorry bringing us back to camp, saying that he wanted me to do him a favour at the weekend. I had agreed to visit him at the officers' mess at 8pm. The call to Ann was fortunate because her friend, Winnie, wanted Ann to stay with her for two nights and help with the cutting out of a suit for Winnie to wear at a wedding. After the call I felt guilty because I had readily agreed to stay on camp, without mentioning the possibility of being with Groves. I was conscious of the fact that Ann felt awkward giving me the Winnie news so soon after the bombshell about Skegness.

My chat with Groves was most unexpected. He was looking for a babysitter to mind his five year old son while he and his wife went to a show and a hotel in London, to celebrate their anniversary. It would mean getting a twenty-four-hour pass and staying overnight at their flat. I could hardly refuse when he added that I was the only person he knew who he would trust doing the job. We agreed that I should not tell anyone of the arrangement and that I would cycle into Ramsgate on Saturday morning and have lunch with them, to allow the boy to get used to me.

Fortunately, Saturday was a sunny day. I don't know what I would have done if I had arrived soaked at their place. I had a pocket full of sweets from the NAAFI and intended to use them if the boy got fed up with me. Gerald and Mary Groves welcomed me with the news that we were all going to the beach for cricket, their son David's favourite game. This turned out to be a great idea, giving me the opportunity to buy him an ice cream. We were immediate friends, and David was quite relaxed about the idea of me looking after him. Back at the flat, I was taken on a tour of the rooms and shown where all the food was stored. I could use anything and I discovered that David loved beans on toast, so there would be no problems over food.

The whole scheme was successful. We played board games until bedtime and I heard nothing from him until he woke me at 7am to go to the beach. We left a note for Gerald inviting them to join us if they returned before us. But David soon tired and we were home when his parents arrived. The icing on the cake was the realisation that an envelope that Gerald gave to me as I left, contained three one pound notes, nearly enough to pay for my holiday in Brighton.

Ann was delighted when I told her on the telephone about the three pounds but she laughed and reminded me of my comments relating to national service officers, like Margaret's John.

28th June, 1950

My own darling future wife,
When you receive this letter we shall have been going out for two years. It certainly doesn't seem as long as that, does it? You have made my life so enjoyable, that the time has flown. Thank you very much for being so kind to me all this time and thank you again for going out with me at all. I have always said that it was providence that brought us together at that speedway meeting and I have never regretted it.
I laughed when you told me that Margaret had permed her hair. Don't do it to your hair, It is beautiful as it is, naturally curly.
I enclose my ration card for the week in Brighton, so you can send it to Mrs. Richardson with yours. That ought to please her. I am really excited about our holiday. The good news is that I have got three extra days added to the front of my leave, as a bonus for doing the guard of honour.
Keep safe and well darling. I would hate anything to go wrong with the holiday.
With all the love from your future husband,
Arthur xxx

The last few days before my leave, dragged. Derek had planned his leave to coincide with mine. Being crafty, he didn't want to be responsible for cleaning the billet on his own. Both of our leaves qualified for travel warrants, and, for a change, we were able to travel to London in style, instead of hitch-hiking. My warrant was an authority to travel to Brighton, via London, making a great saving on our holiday cost. Ann had planned to travel by coach, but fortunately had not bought our tickets.

The two extra days enabled me to get my holiday clothes together while Ann was at work. I hadn't given much thought to what I would be taking and consequently my mother had to do some last minute washing and ironing. This came as a surprise to her because I had not warned her that I was going on holiday with Ann alone.

"You be careful," was the only comment she made. We never indulged in long conversations in our house and I seldom took Ann home to meet my family. Most of my mother's references to Ann were, "I know where you were last night. I saw you in the Regal

Cinema," or wherever she had been on duty with the St. Johns Ambulance Brigade. If Ann and I were planning to go to a cinema, Ann would always ask where my mum or dad was likely to be on duty, before we decided where to go.

I was not very well organised on the Saturday morning. We had planned to catch the 10.30 am train from Clapham Junction to Brighton, which meant leaving Ann's house by 9.30 am. But at 8.30 am I found that the case that I hoped to use was split. Mum had another small case and I had no choice but to accept it, resulting in the necessity for me to wear my raincoat over my sports jacket, even though the sun was shining. I also had to go without a spare pair of trousers. I left home without saying goodbye, cross and hot.

Ann was amused by my predicament but her mother saved my blushes by offering me another case, large enough to pack the raincoat. So our holiday didn't start in a relaxed fashion. Both her mum and dad said, 'have a good time,' but I knew what they meant and my embarrassment was plain to see.

Having turned and waved to her parents at the corner of Greenway, Ann grabbed my hand, giving it a squeeze. As we waited for a 118 bus for the station, my aggressiveness left me and I couldn't help commenting on her lovely summer dress.

"I saved this one for you. I knew you would like the buttons at the front."

"I hadn't noticed," I lied, "but the colour suits you."

The journey to Brighton was uneventful. I failed to find an empty carriage, which disappointed me, but we pretended to be concentrating on the views, with the occasional comment. At Brighton station I asked a newspaper seller for directions to our guest house, and discovered that we had to get a bus to Hove. As we walked up a side street from the promenade, I suddenly became nervous, not knowing whether Mrs. Richardson was expecting us to be married. I hadn't told Ann that her son Jim had suggested that we should buy a ring.

My concern was unfounded because a smiling, matronly lady greeted us before I had a chance to ring the doorbell.

"Ah, Miss Cobbett and your boyfriend from RAF Sandwich. Come in. I see you're not married, separate cases. You can leave them in your rooms and then come back in time for cooked tea at six 'o clock. Breakfast will be at eight thirty each day and nine on Sunday. Rooms must be vacated daily between ten and four thirty. You can have a bath twice in the week by arrangement. And one strict rule, keep to your own rooms. I'm sure your mother would agree, Miss Cobbett, eh? It's best if we understand each other. If you go out in the evening, the front door is locked at ten."

As I struggled up the narrow stairs with the two cases, we got the fits of the giggles. Mrs. Richardson unlocked the first door on the second floor, and laughed as she entered.

"Sorry about the squeaky floorboards, but they tell me who's walking about. And the other room has a squeaky door for the same reason."

I changed into my plimsolls and hurried downstairs to wait for Ann, too frightened to see if she was ready. Ann hadn't changed and as we walked to the beach, we both wondered why there had to be so many rules. But neither of us would dare to annoy Mrs. Richardson and we were just too happy to be together for a week. We found a sunny spot against a breakwater that shielded us from the wind and discarded our shoes and socks.

"In my last letter to you darling I said that I couldn't wait to be on holiday with nobody to tell us when to go to bed, or what time to eat, or when we could kiss." I interrupted Ann for a kiss, our first since we left home. "Now we are here," she continued, "nothing has changed."

"We'll just have to make the most of our times like this," and we were silent for ages, our lips vibrating and blotting out any thoughts of disappointment. The incoming tide gave us a sharp reminder that if we were to have tea, we would have to get moving.

Mrs. Richardson showed us the front room where we could wait to be called for meals and where we could get hot chocolate or Horlicks after 9pm before going to bed. Another couple were in there awaiting the call for tea.

"We're Jessie and Alec. Been here a week already. Quite nice here but the food is a bit samey. We've got macaroni cheese tonight and a pudding. You get meat twice a week if you've brought a ration card. We had best end of neck last night. One thing, she likes us down on time for breakfast. Wants us out of the house asap."

"Heck!" I said, "Can you give me a call? I'm Arthur, room three. Ann is in four."

"Oh. So you're not married. Neither are we, but she thinks this is our honeymoon. Quite embarrassing really but we had to say that because of the names on the ration cards. Her son Jim is a mate of mine and he put us up to getting a ring. You'll have no difficulty in the morning;

she has the wireless on in the kitchen and makes sure that we all hear it."

"I know Jim. We shared a billet at RAF Sandwich for a couple of months. I'm still there."

Tea was a strange affair. Alec wanted to talk and I just wanted to finish the meal and get out with Ann. It was all right for him. He was sleeping with his girl but Ann and I would have just two and a half hours together before being separated. Eventually, we excused ourselves and escaped, but forgot to leave our room keys with Mrs. Richardson who came running after us down the road.

"I need to know when you're out. Make sure you're back by ten."

The tide was covering most of the beach but we found a secluded spot under the sea wall that was already home to three other couples. Our approach was unnoticed and at last we could enjoy each other's warmth and words of love. We laughed about Alec and Jessie pretending to be married and Ann said she was glad that we hadn't done the same thing. I told Ann that Jim had made the same point to me, but I thought it was wrong, so I hadn't suggested it. As dusk encompassed us we became more daring, more reckless, but always stopping short of our forbidden goal.

The fear of upsetting Mrs. Richardson on the first evening brought us back from the brink of ecstasy, to reality. Reluctantly, we tidied ourselves, realising that we had sand everywhere. Laughter took over as every item of clothing had to be shaken to avoid taking the beach to the bedroom. On our way home, hand-in-hand, we stopped a dozen times to kiss. We thanked each other for the respect that we had shown. We wanted our love to rise above the temptation to give in.

Back in my own room, I listened to the squeaky floor of the room opposite, and imagined Ann at her most beautiful best, trying to get undressed quietly, but without success. Mrs. Richardson, surely, must be satisfied that we were in our own rooms. I wouldn't be able to face her in the morning if I had betrayed her trust and Christian principles.

Sunday morning didn't go according to plan. We had intended to get the Eastbourne bus and alight at Beachy Head for a walk along the cliffs. One hundred yards from the guesthouse, however, we noticed a Methodist chapel with a welcoming invitation to join the ten thirty service. Although we had never attended a church together, it seemed to be a natural impulse to do so on holiday.

The Beachy Head trip was put off till Monday, and we joined the throngs of day-trippers on the beach. The sun was persistent and when we joined Jessie and Alec for tea, they commented on our red necks and faces. By the morning, both of us were sore and Jessie gave us some calamine lotion which caused heaps of laughter when it dried patchy and pink. The sun though, had had its day and was replaced by rain, heavy rain. A soaking in the morning pointed us in the direction of the cinema for the afternoon. Luckily, we had the back row to ourselves, so the quality of the entertainment on the screen was incidental.

The cost of food at mid-morning was a problem each day, but we found an ice cream parlour on the sea-front and had promised ourselves a treat on the Tuesday of having a knickerbocker glory. The tall wide glasses were filled to over-flowing with fruit, chocolate, cream and ice cream and the thought of being a little extravagant gave us a lot of pleasure.

The Tuesday evening meal was sausages and mash and the main topic of conversation was that sausages were not rationed and we hoped that this meal didn't constitute one of the two meat dishes for the week. Mrs. Richardson overheard our concern and took offence, saying that we were lucky to get such good food, and wiped a crocodile tear from her eye. We all mimicked her after she had left the room and had a good laugh.

The Black Dyke Mills Band was the centre of attraction on the bandstand on Wednesday. The audience had to pay for deckchairs within the confines of the stand, but we could hear quite well by sitting on the promenade wall. To our surprise, one of the pieces played was 'Blaze Away', the signature tune of the Wimbledon Speedway team. It brought back the fond memory of our first meeting two years previously, at the Plough Lane track.

The sun returned on the Friday, allowing us to make the journey to Beachy Head. As we lay for hours on the grassy cliffs, we couldn't believe that our holiday was almost over. Our happiness during the week was obvious and our love had been tested and found to be complete. We had virtually no money, but we didn't seem to demand expensive entertainment. The positive outlook centred around the success of getting a good job when my RAF days ended in two months time, but that would still give us three years before we could reasonably expect to be able to marry.

As I lay on my bed treasuring the thoughts about my darling Ann, and our superb holiday, I reminded myself about her impending Butlins holiday with her workmates. Tomorrow, we would be going home and she deserved that extra treat in a week's time, and I had to respect and trust her. If I endangered our life together by losing faith in her, then it would be my fault, and my loss.

CHAPTER 10

A bit of a bombshell awaited us at Ann's home on our return from Brighton. I was due back at Sandwich on the Monday noon, but Pilot Officer Groves had sent a telegram for me to report to RAF Bawdsey on Sunday afternoon, ready to play the next round for the cricket cup on Monday. It had been sent to my address, but Mum had taken it to Ann's house, knowing that I would go there first.

We had no choice, really, so we consoled ourselves with the memories of a wonderful holiday, unspoilt by any upsets or disagreements, and enjoyed what was left of Saturday. There were the expected questions from Ann's parents and Margaret regarding details of our days and nights away, and after a bout of prodding, Ann snapped.

"Mum, you really don't trust me do you? If we wanted to do anything wrong, we could do it here, without going all the way to Hove. You're embarrassing Arthur." And there were no further comments.

I caught a mid-morning train to Ipswich on Sunday, to ensure that I was sorted out in Bawdsey before tea. The decision paid off because there were no buses from Old Felixstowe to the ferry and I had to walk. There was a queue for the ferry so I remembered an old trick of the trade from my Bawdsey days and caught the eye of Mr. Brinkley, the ferryman.

"Ah, any airmen for RAF Bawdsey, come to the front of the queue, please. We don't want to put our country at risk, do we?"

Pilot Officer Groves had left a message at the guardroom for me to report to him in the officers' mess. I found him enjoying the sun on the terrace and he immediately invited me to join him for a beer, brought to us by the orderly sergeant who assumed that I was a visiting officer in civvies.

"We have the same team as before, and your mates are all billeted in hut five. I guessed that you wouldn't have any cricket gear with you, so I authorised Jack to pick the lock of your wardrobe. Have another beer and we'll forget the small matter of all the cooking equipment that I found in the sports store. You would be for the high jump if Platt knew. Twenty-eight days in Colchester, at least, for the fire risk."

I made a poor attempt at justifying the need to supplement the standard food allocation at Sandwich.

"Look after my son David next Friday night, and I'll forget the packets of food 'borrowed' from the cookhouse for the midnight feasts." We laughed and shook on the deal. "Win the match for us tomorrow, and I'll get you promotion before you get demobbed in September."

The evening was spent in the NAAFI where our team had the place to itself. There were no current courses on site and the majority of the regular staff were on weekend passes until midnight. Derek had returned from leave in time to volunteer to join the travelling supporters' lorry and his presence meant that we consumed a vast amount of liquor.

In fact, the six hours of celebration time in the NAAFI exceeded the time that it took our team to lose the match on the following morning. Having lost the toss, we were put into bat and had no answer to the two fast bowlers of Bawdsey. Our captain stayed at the crease for the longest time, scoring fifteen runs but six of us had our stumps knocked over without scoring and the side capitulated for twenty four. By lunchtime, we were back in the NAAFI, continuing where we had left off on the previous evening. News that the opposition bowlers were county standard cricketers, playing for Cheshire, bore little comfort. We returned to Sandwich in the bumpy station wagon, not only defeated, but annihilated. In my own mind, however, I had the additional loss, that of knowing promotion had been a dream.

14th July, 1950

My own darling Arthur.

What can I say about the holiday? I had been looking forward to it so much, and then it passed so quickly. But it was even more enjoyable than I dared to hope. .You were so thoughtful every day and you always had ideas of what to do when the weather made us change our minds.

I'm sorry that Mum embarrassed you so much when she kept prying into what we got up to at night. She doesn't seem to understand that we can have respect for each other. I just want to be with you and in your arms for ever.

It was lovely sitting on the beach, even in the cold wind, planning our lives together. I now want our wedding day to come as soon as we have saved enough money. It won't happen if we keep on having knickerbockers glories. But it was fun daring to have two on our holiday. Greedy, aren't we?

I know that you are worried about next week when I shall be in Skegness, but after such a lovely holiday, I shall be true to you.

With all my love, from your future wife, Ann.

Ann was right about my worries, but I was determined to keep to Derek's advice and not 'rock the boat'. I was being helped by the increased number of aircraft manoeuvres, demanding longer watches and giving me less free time. I spent the weekend of Ann's departure, in Ramsgate, staying overnight at P/O Groves' house, child-minding. This gave me the opportunity to write a long letter of love, ready to send to Skegness as soon as I got the address. The overnight stay proved to be fruitful, netting me another £5 and two good meals.

Although Ann wrote just as she was about to go on holiday, it was Thursday before I heard from her, and then I got three letters together. By that time, my thoughts were running wild, wondering whether her friends were enticing her to go off the rails. One of the letters, a souvenir letter card from Butlins, was loving and happy, leading me to add a postscript to my prepared letter. On reflection, I wished that I hadn't, because the innuendoes about her dancing with other fellows was too near the truth in my own mind, and may have annoyed Ann.

My excitement of getting to London Victoria coach station on the Saturday evening in time to meet Ann on her return, was cut short by a headline in the Evening Standard predicting an immediate increase of six months to national service. I was devastated and still in a state of shock when Ann's coach arrived. The news took all of the pleasure out of seeing Ann and our journey home was a sombre affair.

"You haven't asked me about my holiday yet." We were sitting silently, hand-in-hand on the train to Raynes Park. "Aren't you interested?"

Of course I was interested. I was frightened to hear what I would rather not know. I had made up my mind to avoid any deep interrogation. I kept hearing Derek's advice, 'don't rock the boat.'

"Sorry, darling, I was miles away, trying to escape from the RAF," I lied. Then, after an awkward search for the right words, "was the food good?"

"Oh not bad, but a bit samey each day. Plenty of it though. You should have seen Pam. Every meal, she hid food in her bag and took it back to our room, in case we were hungry. We had two chalets between us. I shared with Doreen. She's a card. Kept getting tangled up with a feller at the dances and then taking him back for a snog. Embarrassing, really, I had to hang around one evening till he'd left."

I guessed that would happen and hearing about it sent me into an uncomfortable silence again.

You don't think that I did it, do you? I love you too much and although the girls told me I was silly, I really didn't let you down, Arthur. I danced with a chap who wore a sports jacket like yours, but he didn't look as handsome as you. And he wasn't interested in anything but dancing and eating. He never tried to kiss me, honest."

We spent the weekend trying to discover a small measure of comfort from the fact that the news about the national service had not been confirmed, and might not even happen.

The morale back at Sandwich was at an all time low. The national service airmen were subjected to constant banter from the regulars who were not affected by the possible change. Discipline suffered on camp as many tried to drown their sorrows in the NAAFI bar, leading to fights with the long-term airmen. In an attempt to defuse the situation, the CO paraded the entire camp personnel, and called for an adult approach to the news that still had not been confirmed. He offered a concession that the dining standards would be enhanced immediately, and work rotas would be reviewed. But his concluding assessment left us in no doubt that any continuation of the friction prompted by alcohol would result in camp concessions being withdrawn. The threat would include the closure of the NAAFI bar and off site leave passes being curtailed.

The fracas was short-lived and the resigned feeling of 'there's nothing we can do about it' took over. The friendship between regulars and national servicemen returned to its natural state. In fact, the only mark that distinguished a longer-serving man from the eighteen month airman was the worn appearance of his uniform.

But the possibility of being separated from Ann for another six months, especially when we were so close to the end of my stint, hung over me. Although I enjoyed the challenge of 'beating the system' by any means available, this was no substitute for getting home. The child-minding for Groves could be lucrative but my wings had been clipped by his discovery of my catering habits in the sports store.

Derek wanted to take a chance with the cooking, but I had too much to lose by risking my relationship with Groves.

The August Bank Holiday weekend loomed, but no leave passes were granted due to operations planned for the Friday and Sunday. Ann and her mother, however, decided to catch a special excursion train to Ramsgate on the Saturday and I spent the day with them. They had heard about the Viking ship but we were surprised at the popularity of the exhibition. The highlight of the day was our picnic on the beach in hot sunshine. I was sent to get some cornet ice creams and on my return, I was greeted with the beautiful sight of Ann in her swimming costume. Her mother had sent me away to save my embarrassment while Ann changed.

7th August, 1950

My own darling Ann.
Thank you for such a lovely day in Ramsgate. As I am writing this, you will still be in the train going home. I don't envy you because it must be stifling hot with no fresh air. You were such a darling all day and I loved you so much, especially when you played around in the sand. There's a pile of sand in the billet from when I took my shirt off.
I hope your mum enjoyed the day and that she saw how happy we are, together.
It's exciting about Margaret getting her engagement ring. I hope that the one we get for you will be just as nice-looking, even though it may not cost as much.
Have a good time at the 'Follies Bergere' on Monday. You did well to get circle seats for 10/6.
I must rush now to get the evening collection at the post office.
With all my love , from your very happy future husband,
Arthur.

The CO was right when he said that he would be reviewing the operation rotas. The result was that suddenly, we were doing extended watches and on two successive days, I worked 3.15am to 7.15, 9am to 12.30 and 2pm to 5.30. The logic from the CO's point of view was that if we were too tired in the evenings, we wouldn't spend time in the NAAFI, and there would be no fighting. But the food certainly improved. Tables were decorated with flowers, not that we could eat them, and bacon appeared on the menu at breakfast three times per week. It was streaky bacon, but, with tomato sauce and doorstep slices of bread, it made lovely sandwiches, and a change from marmalade. At tea, we were suddenly allowed to have two vegetables with potatoes.

22nd August, 1950

My own darling Ann,
It's 7.15am and it's so hot and humid. Yesterday was over 80 degrees. We couldn't sleep so six of us went down to Sandwich Bay for a paddle. We were soon mucking about and one of the blokes got out of his depth and fell off his pedalo. He couldn't swim and luckily I heard him screaming. But as you know, I can't swim so Derek and Bernard got to him just in time and saved the pedalo as well. None of us had any costumes on.
Last night we went to Ramsgate to see Danny Kaye in 'The Inspector General'. When we came out at 6.15 I remembered that I needed stamps for your letter. The stamp machine at the post office was empty so we had to hunt around. Even when I found one, I had to pay three whole pennies because the halfpenny machine was empty. So I hope that I caught the post.
We then had egg ,chips and peas at the Cyprus Restaurant before catching the 7.15pm bus back to camp and straight to bed.
I now have only thirty eight days before I've finished with this mob, fingers crossed. Then I shall be with you forever. I love you so much and want to be with you until I die.
With all my love, from your future husband,
Arthur.

The term, 'getting de-mob happy' was a feeling that one gets in the RAF when the day of leaving the service was drawing close; and I was getting that feeling. I was becoming at ease with the world and the only cloud hanging over me was the possibility of the six months extension. The news had gone very quiet on the subject. I took a short weekend pass so that I could enjoy a coach trip for a cricket match at Littlehampton and I could sense that Ann was as relaxed as me at the prospect that I would soon be at home with her. It was a very happy coach for the return journey after winning the match convincingly. I must have consumed more alcohol than usual because I started singing, which was something unheard of in company that I respected.

I was conscious of the comments of Ernest Waine, my music master at school, whose advice rankled in my ears whenever I burst into song, 'Arthur, don't ever try and sing for money. You'll embarrass the audience.'

"Annie, Annie, give me your answer do, I'm half crazy, all for the love of you"

Ann remarked that it was the first occasion that I had sung to her. Spurred on, and holding her hands, I gazed into her eyes and proceeded to risk our friendship.

"It won't be a stylish marriage, I can't afford a carriage. But you'll look sweet, upon the seat, of a bicycle made for two."

"That's about all we shall be able to afford, she laughed, "and I expect that your dad will cut the sandwiches for the wedding breakfast, and guess what he'll make them with? Beetroot." And we both had fits of the giggles because I was renowned for taking beetroot sandwiches whenever we went cycling.

Ann accompanied me to London on the Sunday, to wave goodbye as I boarded the Sandwich train. For once, there were no tears, just a formal acceptance of a brief period of being apart.

Derek was due to be demobbed on 30th September, the same day as me. We had similar interests as far as life was concerned. We had made the most of the compulsory service and shared the fears of losing our loved ones. It was now the 30th August and as we sat contemplating the future whilst supping a beer in the NAAFI, we guessed that we would get just one more weekend leave before going for good. We had stood up for each other on many occasions. Both had benefited from the mutual friendship. Now, we just had to survive the last thirty days.

They call it sod's law. As we were preparing to go on watch the following morning, the wireless broadcast a statement from the War Department that the Prime Minister, Clement Attlee would be speaking to the nation at 6pm that evening. We all knew the content of his message. We were going to be the chopping block of the cold war. Derek and I were about to hear the dreaded news that the King needed us to defend him for a bit longer.

The day dragged like no other day. Nobody was a bit interested in the fact that the aircraft going east across our operation table at fifteen thousand feet, was a friendly aircraft. We wanted to know the horrible truth.

At five forty five there wasn't a soul walking about Stonar House, RAF Sandwich. Every airman, NCO and officer was glued to a wireless. There was plenty of noise coming from each of the billets as airmen screamed abuse about the government, Russia and even Sgt Platt. We wanted to know but we weren't going to like it. Then it started. The squeaky voice of the Prime Minister wished us a good evening. He then outlined the current world situation and the challenge facing us. And then, the bombshell.

"Consequently, we need all the resources we have, to be at our command. All national service personnel still on active service as at 1st October, 1950, will of necessity, extend their tour of duty by six months. Good night."

Clement Attlee had never inspired me as a minister or orator. But suddenly, I wanted to hug him and kiss him. Instead, Derek and I hugged each other, not daring to believe what we had just heard. It took minutes to sink in that we were about to escape from this existence, after all.

Our natural instinct was to go and shout on the parade ground outside, but as we ventured through our door to the quadrangle, all hell was let loose. The realisation of something that had been inevitable for several weeks was hard for many affected airmen to accept. As we stood there, we realised that a mob was gathering, sorting out those of us who were due for release before the end of September.

Then we heard the cry that billet 13a, our home, would be last out. In a panic, Derek and I locked our door and rushed from the back of the building into the fields. Our only thoughts were for survival and that meant getting away until the heat had subsided. We were frightened. Our friends had turned into animals.

We made our way round to the guardroom, hoping that there would be some form of protection available. To our amazement, we found that it was manned by two 'snowdrops', RAF police, a breed never before seen at Sandwich. We ventured in, giving our names and our fears. Their response was to ridicule us. But as we were about to leave, the telephone rang. Somebody was reporting that billet 13a was being ransacked. Having ascertained that it was our billet, we were hustled back into the security of the guardroom.

By midnight, order had been restored and we were allowed to view the damage. As we approached our billet, escorted by one of the police, the cat-calls from the other room mates told us that we had better keep quiet and not retaliate. We recognised our beds, bent and buckled in the quadrangle. Bedclothes were everywhere. The door had been forced and wardrobes emptied. A fire extinguisher had shed its foam all round the room. Luckily, there had been no fire. Sgt Platt greeted us.

"I'll be glad when you have both gone. I get nothing but trouble from you. You always have excuses for not doing your share of fatigues. Now this."

"Oh, stop crying sergeant, you know you enjoy trying to beat us. You're not up to it." Derek was having his last dig at poor old Platt. "Now where do you want us to sleep tonight? And can we sort this lot out in the morning, instead of fatigues?"

"Pilot Officer Groves has instructed me to put you both in room two in the officers mess for tonight. God help you if you dirty that place. Report to me in the morning for some new gear."

Peace had been restored and Stonar House went to sleep.

CHAPTER 11

There was an eerie feeling at breakfast on the morning following the ransacking of our room. Derek and I didn't exactly arrive holding hands, but we were prepared for anything. As the pre-lunch flying operations had been cancelled, only a few airmen had bothered to get up for breakfast and they all looked not guilty. Nobody approached us and we enjoyed a cooked meal in peace.

We decided to venture back to Room 13a and size up the situation. We understood the jealousy of those who had been caught on the wrong side of October 1st and we knew how we would have felt. We were not expecting the scene that confronted us, however, as we turned the corner towards our room. All the contents were piled high, outside the room, and the sounds of scrubbing and singing were emanating from within.

Unbeknown to us, the 'snowdrops' police had taken action overnight and had rounded up two ringleaders of the fracas, both of whom had willingly admitted their actions. The CO had intervened personally when the police were going to arrest the men. Sensing that he could be short of radar operators if he lost the men, he instructed Sgt Platt to ensure the men cleaned up the mess and place them on a charge for wilful damage to Air Ministry property. The police, however, were expecting a full court martial of the two.

To our surprise, the operatic entertainment was being voiced by the 'clown prince', the comedian who took Rosie off my hands, when I had been faced with the delicate situation in Cliftonville. Codger, another friend, was the other

"Come on Prince," I called, "surely you didn't do this. You're both in the cricket team. I thought we were mates."

"Too right I did," and then, after moving the step ladder to allow us to enter, "jammy sods. I missed the cut by two weeks." He released a string of expletives that probably made him feel better. "We've got another hour to clean the room, then we're in front of the CO. Could even go to Colchester if the snowdrops get their way."

"That won't happen, Prince. Derek and I will come and put a good word in, for you. I'll go and see Platt."

At that moment, Sgt Platt strutted into the billet, confident that he was about to nail another successful charge to his record. He eyed the work being carried out.

"Ok you two. Another hour to finish this room, but you'd better get your own place sorted out, as well. You may not be seeing it again for a while. Six weeks, probably."

"Sarge, Derek and I want to be at the charge hearing. This was only a prank that got out of hand."

"Don't talk balls. Damage to property. If you're outside the CO at 10, you may get in, but I doubt it, if I have my way."

Well, Sgt Platt didn't get his way. Derek and I donned our best blue uniform for the charge parade and the Station Admin Officer ruled that the accused had every right to have submissions on his behalf. The CO appeared to be in one of his cross moods, which was quite unusual. But after expounding at length about the need for discipline and the cost of equipment, it became apparent that he was more concerned about putting on a strict face in front of the snowdrop policeman who brought the charge, and whose assertion was that the two airmen were inciting a riot over the news of the six months extension. Eventually, the CO asked me to list the damage to my property.

"Sir, we have no complaint about our personal gear. We often play jokes on each other and we accept that this affair was in retaliation for something I did to Prince. We are all friends and they have cleaned our room. Prince was due for demob just after 1st October, so this is why he over-reacted. We are all prepared to share the cost of the damage, sir."

Platt made a quiet comment that brought a rebuke from the CO. There was a shuffling of papers and a whispered conversation between the CO and the Admin officer.

"If there are no further submissions, I'll give my ruling." Prince gave me a wink as the CO continued. "There will be no court martial. But you two have not behaved in a manner befitting this station. The severity of your actions deserve a similar response from the authorities, but in view of mitigating circumstances of your extended national service requirements, you will be confined to camp for fourteen days and will forfeit two weeks pay. But let it be known that this is not a precedent for others to act stupidly."

We left the office in disbelief, as did Sgt Platt.

"I'll get you bastards before long," he said, "You can sort out the whereabouts of beds to replace your broken ones."

Clown Prince was waiting for us back at our billet.

"I owe you one for that Lefty. Leave the beds to us. We'll sort it out. Sorry if you've lost anything. See you in the NAAFI tonight." And for once, he kept his word. Our room returned to its former state, and we didn't ask where the bedding and furniture came from. After a few beers we were all mates and the previous night was history. The clown became his old self again, joking about everything.

"Tell yer what, Lefty, as I'm boxed in here for two weeks, you can have Rosie once a week. How's that? Can't be more generous than that. She'll be begging for it. Not seen her since Saturday."

"No chance. Not putting my health at risk. I'll leave you to tell her why you can't see her. Anyhow, it'll give her time to have a bath before you get her again." And we all laughed.

10th September, 1950

My own darling Arthur, who will soon be with me for ever. ...

Thank you for the lovely weekend. You did well cycling home from camp, but it solved the problem of getting your bike home.

It felt funny when we said goodbye last night, because I wasn't upset. Sometimes in the past, I have stood on the railway platform and cried after saying bye bye. Perhaps it's the fact that we are now only three weeks away from being together, and never to be parted again for the rest of our lives.

I enjoyed talking about your demob. You will need to buy some clothes, such as socks pants, shirts and a suit. But I would like to buy a raincoat for you. We'll have a smashing day shopping.

I got even better news when I arrived at work. I've been given a five shillings per week rise. Aren't I a clever girl?

I am so excited, with all my love to the best man in the world,
Ann.

Both Derek and I were getting demob-happy. Neither of us had a civvy job organised and Derek had no idea what he wanted to do. It was while we were discussing the possibilities, when he sowed seeds of doubt in my mind about my own plans. I had received the Pitmans certificate to get me a place in Goldsmiths Teachers Training College, but I hadn't considered what was I going to do for money during the three years college work. I lay awake most of the next night, with my head in a whirl. At breakfast, I made up my mind.

"That's it. I am not going to teach for a career. You're right, Derek, as always. Money is the root of all evil, as the song goes, but we shall never get married if I don't start putting some money in the Post Office Account. Ann is trying hard and I'll have to take a chance that she will understand that my heart isn't behind teaching grubby little children."

We were still at breakfast when we were both summoned to the CO's office.

"I've just had this signal from above. Flying ops are being stepped up in October and I'm going to need every airman I can get my hands on to see me through. I've been authorised to offer the two of you special arrangements if you will stay on for an extra month. It won't count as national service and you won't have to stay any longer. You will get the pay of a corporal. What do you think?"

"I can't, sir," Derek lied, "I start my new job on 1st October."

"Neither can I, sir," I lied equally. "I am going to the Goldsmiths Teachers Training College and their course has already started."

"Ok chaps, Neither would I in your position. You'd better call in the admin office and sort out what you have to do to escape camp. See me before you go."

We saluted, casually, with an air of not belonging to the formality of the service, keeping straight faces until we were out of ear-shot.

"Bloody liar, Lefty, you could lie for England. Come on, let's see what admin can do for us."

Admin had plenty to say. I played snooker with Fingers Carter one of the staff, and he was particularly miffed at me getting out. He had missed demob by two months.

"This form has to be signed by all Sections listed. You'll need to go to Manston to see the pay bods and the Medical Officer. Clean pants that day. And it's West Malling for your kit parade. You keep one uniform to do your 'H' Reserve training but you'll pay for any missing items. Leave admin till last and we sign when you've been everywhere else. I'll try and delay our signature until after the 1st October. Then you'll have to stay in. Ha ha."

We went to the NAAFI for a mug of tea and studied the form. Our first priority would be to get the MT section to arrange transport to the other camps. But one signature that could cause problems was that of Sgt. Platt. If he was reminded that we were due to escape, he would give us all the latrine cleaning and guard duties. We decided that we would dodge him for as long as possible. The thought of this intrigue added spice to our task of signature-hunting; one last chance to put one over him.

20th September, 1950

My dearest, darling Ann,
Thank you for the surprise goodies that arrived today. The lads thank you as well. The crumble that your mum made was crumbly and your shortbread was short, but we had a great feast. You have no need to worry about your cooking, darling. Just keep baking your shortbread when we're married and I'll be more than satisfied.
Today should be a day off, but we had a parade for one of the flight sergeants to be presented with the British Empire Medal for his work getting this station back in operation after the fire. Then, we had an emergency watch for a rehearsal for a London fly-past next Friday. So, if you hear a load of fighters and bombers going over, you'll know that we are involved.
I've counted the number of letters that you have written to me. Can you believe that you've written 205 which means about £2.2s 0d in stamps. If you hadn't written, we could have got married one week earlier.
Only nine days to go. I cannot believe it.
With all my love forever, from your husband-to-be,
Arthur.

The Medical Officer was a comedian.

"My job is to ensure that your report shows that you are in a healthier state than when you joined up. Let's see now, er, you are one stone heavier than eighteen months ago. So, we have been overfeeding you. Your blood pressure is not in the danger zone, so there's been little stress and plenty of exercise. You still don't have gonorrhoea or syphilis. So you've kept your powder dry. Perhaps you haven't served on a mixed station. Still, your mummy will be proud of you."

Another signature required was that of Pilot Officer Groves, for the sports section.

"I'll get that one for both of us," I volunteered. "I need to tell him about the split cricket bat." I lied again. Derek was unaware of my child-minding and I wanted to keep it that way. We were both crawlers but he could think that I had gone too far. Groves was pleased to see me and was surprised at my imminent departure. He offered a farewell dinner with his family, but I decided to sever the relationship while it was still secret.

Flying operations were stepped up for the weekend and everyone had three shifts per day. Morale amongst the airmen destined to enjoy an extended stay was painfully low in the ops room, resulting in apathy creeping into the standard of work produced. On several occasions the officer in charge had to scream at plotters who were placing the directional arrows on the ops table incorrectly, indicating that an aircraft was flying backwards. Human error sometimes crept into the work and would normally provoke laughter, even amongst the officers, but the atmosphere was tense. On both days I took over fifteen minutes early from one particular plotter who was close to being put on a charge for sloppy work, just to allow him to go outside for a smoke.

On the Monday, my last week, there was a definite shortage of radar operators following the busy weekend, and I volunteered to do the morning shift in the radar room. Although fighter plotters had no training for this aspect of the work, we often jumped at a chance to add a bit of variety to our day. The radar equipment was housed in a different building to the ops table, so, provided that the information from the radar screens was translated correctly to the ops room, the officers would be unaware of the operators involved.

On my return to my billet, I was greeted with a note from Sgt. Platt that he had placed me on guard duty for the Tuesday and Wednesday. It was signed, "get out of that, enjoy your demob." So he had grasped the last laugh, but in doing so, he had saved me from the problem of where would the money come from, if I had to pay for celebrations in the pub.

It also gave me the opportunity to write my final letter of love to Ann.

27th September, 1950

Positively the last showing of ... 'Stonar House, RAF Sandwich, Kent.'

My very true and very dear Ann,
Well darling, it has been a very long time, but at last, after writing this letter, I can put my paper and pen into that lovely brown writing

case that you gave me, and not worry any more as to whether I shall have time to write the next day. Isn't it a lovely thought?

I have a lot to thank you for. It is strange how many chaps come back to camp after leave and say that they have lost their girl friend, either because of their continued absence, or because one or other has stopped loving the other.

But, thanks to you, darling I have never had that happen to me, and therefore I have been able to enjoy the RAF,(such as it is.) I have been able to return to camp knowing that you were as eager to see me the following week, as I was, to see you. That is a wonderful feeling to have when you are separated from your loved one. It made me feel that I was wanted.

But I had plenty to remind me of you besides the constant memories of our happy holidays and outings together. Your smiling photo has always hung over my bed and I have never let an evening go by without kissing you goodnight. It comforted me, and left me with thoughts of you, probably tucked up and asleep in your bed at home. All the boys have admired it but I'm sure none of them can know how sweet and kind the real Ann is.

I'm sorry the biro you gave me didn't last to the end. Darling, it was such a nice present and I could rely on it. I shall always remember the occasion when you gave it to me at High Wycombe, together with the note, 'I thank God – for he made you mine and gave me your love.'

Darling, our absence has made our love grow stronger, and I'm sure it will always remain strong. Our parting has ended now, and that makes me very happy. Happy because I shall be able to see your pretty face with its blue sparkling eyes and lovely hair every evening. It will be like old times meeting you under the clock in the evenings, after work.

I want to thank you for being so very true to me all this time. Without you my life would be nothing. I shall always love and cherish you my sweetheart for being such a generous, pretty, and in every way, a lovely girl. I am so proud to walk along the road with you because you know how to dress and look so beautiful.

Please keep on loving me Ann and if I am worthy of you, will you still consent to be my wife? I shall do my best to keep you happy. My love for you will never dwindle; my heart is yours.

From your ever-true, husband to be, who cannot live without you,
  Arthur.

Thursday was packing day and both Derek and I were surprised at the amount of rubbish that we had accumulated. It had been confirmed that we would be liable for 'H' reserve training for three years, but current policy indicated that we could expect to be summoned for a two week course in the third year. Consequently, we had to sign for our working uniform and maintain it in full order. My immediate concern was that I had to squeeze it into my kitbag and one case, with a mountain of other clothing and knick-knacks. It proved to be an impossible task and eventually I succumbed to posting a parcel of bulky items to myself at home, leaving me with a lighter load to carry.

We had obtained all the clearance certificates and as flying had been cancelled for the weekend, we could collect our passes to leave camp on the Friday afternoon.

The evening had been set aside for the last booze-up and thirty airmen happened to be passing the NAAFI when we started the first round of pints. It was customary on these occasions for the demob airman to stand the first two rounds of drinks and then there would be a kitty. But there was a sudden change of plan when I was called to the officers' mess to see Pilot Officer Groves.

"Couldn't let you go without saying best of luck with your new life and hope that your young lady turns out to be a good wife. Here's something for the kitty to ease the pocket pain. Thanks for all you've done for us."

I left with £5 which I handed to the NAAFI steward.

"That should give us a good start tonight," and all the airmen within earshot cheered. It was a good night, with no sarcastic comments about our release. Eventually, Derek and I staggered from the bar at closing time, and willingly sunk into our squeaky pits for the last time.

The last day dawned, 29th September, 1950. Ann's photo was the first thing I saw and we would be together that evening. But I had not anticipated the difficulty of saying 'good-bye' to so many mates in the camp. Bernard, Johnny, Crabby, Mitch, the Clown, whose hand-shake was so genuine that it hurt. Three of the cricket team wanted me to turn up for their next match. Somebody even posted a note under our door, 'Lucky sods, but thanks for your company. Enjoy your life after this hell.' And it was signed by about a dozen men. Even Sgt Platt entered the mess at breakfast time, something he had never done to our knowledge.

"All the best lads. Lucky bastards. I'm glad I won't have to listen to your excuses for not working, anymore." And he shook hands and left.

During my life up to that point, 'good-byes' had not meant very much. It usually meant that we would meet again soon. But now, this was different. Without me realising it, the RAF had taught me three things, respect for the King, not to be fussy over food, and, more importantly, the power of comradeship. These were all men who would support me through thick and thin. We all helped each other when someone was in difficulty. We all needed each other. I was leaving those true friends, with little prospect of ever seeing them again.

One more visit to the admin office to collect two weeks ration cards and our precious travel warrants and we were off to the guardhouse to sign out. To our complete surprise, the ration wagon was parked outside, bedecked with a make-shift banner scribbled along the side, 'The Last Escapees from RAF Sandwich'.

"Jump in lads, I'll take you to the station. Can't have you civilians carrying those heavy cases."

Derek and I travelled in silence most of the way to London Bridge. We promised that we would keep in touch and thanked each other for all the good times. We stood on the London Bridge platform not knowing how to say goodbye. I'm sure that I repeated my intention to write when I had settled down, but we knew inside our hearts that a future meeting was quite unlikely. We both had our lives to sort out. It had been a good partnership and both were grateful to the other. And we parted, without even looking back. I'd lost another genuine friend.

If I hurried, I could get to Oxford Street in time to see Ann leaving her dressmaking sweat-shop. I struggled with my kitbag and case and arrived with five minutes to spare. And there she was. Our embrace was hard and long, shared with all her friends who wanted to share our happiness. Two of the girls called a taxi, loaded my gear into it and paid the driver to take us to Waterloo station. What a wonderful start to the rest of our life together.

But our celebrations were a little premature. Three days into my demob leave I was having my usual lie-in when my mother brought a telegram to me. To my horror, it was from Admin at Sandwich. 'Air

Ministry confirms that demobilisation leave forms part of national service. Consequently, you are required to serve a further six months until 29th March,1951. Report back to RAF Sandwich by 0800hrs 16th October 1950. Written confirmation of this telegram will follow. Acknowledge receipt of this telegram.'

"What are you going to do?" asked my mother.

"I'm too dumbfounded to think." Then, after at least thirty seconds consideration, "I'll ignore it."

But the worry lingered all day and when Ann returned from work I tried to conceal the disaster. Ann persisted about my quietness and eventually, I showed her the tatty bit of yellow paper that was at the root of my mood. When she stopped crying we talked of nothing else, but concluded that we would have no option, other than put up with it.

Tuesday's post brought another RAF style envelope, obviously the formal confirmation of our future unhappiness. I opened it reluctantly, not wanting to read the contents.

2nd October,1950

A/C 1 Allwright, Fighter Plotter.
You were expected to telephone Sandwich yesterday to challenge the decision in our telegram. Had you done so, I could have told you that we, in the admin office were pulling your leg and just wanted to return the jokes that you played on us on April 1st. Do you remember? Max was almost charged with wasting officers' time.

Anyhow, we hope we didn't spoil your day. We enclose your ID card that you left behind. Enjoy your leave and life thereafter. Cheerio, Johnny and Bernard.

Words cannot describe my relief. I rushed round to Ann's mother to tell her. Fortunately, she knew the telephone number of Ann's employer and I ran to the phone box at the end of the road. The grumpy woman who answered said that personal calls were not allowed but agreed to pass on my message at lunch time.

Ann's homecoming that evening was a re-enactment of the first night of my demob leave. We could at last believe that we would never again have to suffer the pain of being parted. She arrived home, armed with copies of the three London evening papers, The Evening News, The Star, and Evening Standard.

"We'll go through these tonight, and see what jobs we can find."

Ann and her parents supported the change of direction away from teaching. All we had to do was to find that attractive advert that may lead to the golden egg. Ann pointed to a half page entry in the Evening Standard.

"Clerks required in the Commercial Department of the British Electricity Authority. Salary £225 pa."

Stability returned to our lives. At last, I could contribute to our bottom drawer.

EPILOGUE

My service to the King and my country had been properly executed and I had contributed to the national defence and our recognised strength in the world. But the experience had also been kind to me. At the age of eighteen, few men are lucky enough to absorb the lessons that the RAF had taught me. I have already mentioned the three major advantages of service life, loyalty to the King, comradeship and overcoming food fads. Mixing with people from various walks of life, from the poorest to the well-heeled fraternity, opened my eyes to the unfairness of society. Consequently, I became more thankful for what I had. One officer unwittingly gave me the best advice that anyone could have. When I challenged a certain plan that gave some airmen more than others, he said, quite sincerely, 'Arthur, if you want to enjoy life, then you will have to accept that life is not meant to be fair.'

But the reader of this autobiography is also entitled to learn of the outcome of my relationship with Ann, who figured so prominently throughout my story. It was she who kept me going at times when I felt very low, cold and down-trodden. It was the knowledge of her faithfulness that made me overcome the serious jealousy that hounded me during the early months of our being apart.

We became formally engaged after I had summoned all my courage to ask her father for permission to marry her. The marriage took place in Raynes Park, SW London, on 29th August, 1953, when we enjoyed the fulfilment of our physical desires after five years of courting. Two removals in the Cheshire area to suit my employers culminated in me ending my salaried occupation in 1990. By this time we had settled into a delightful home that would see out the rest of our years. Our castle is a country lodge in Kent.

With two children, seven grandchildren and four great grandchildren, all of whom we adore, our happiness is complete. This happiness is not born of wealth; quite the opposite. It is our comradeship, adherence to our wedding vows and not being fussy that has pulled us through. I wonder where I learned the importance of that?

29th August, 1953

Lightning Source UK Ltd.
Milton Keynes UK
UKOW050319270613

212876UK00003B/869/P